The Mom's Guide to Earning and Saving Thousands on the Internet

The Mom's Guide to Earning and Saving Thousands on the Internet

BARB WEBB

WITH

MAUREEN HECK

McGraw·Hill

New York   Chicago   San Francisco   Lisbon   London   Madrid   Mexico City
Milan   New Delhi   San Juan   Seoul   Singapore   Sydney   Toronto

The **McGraw·Hill** Companies

Library of Congress Cataloging-in-Publication Data

Webb, Barbara, 1969-
      The mom's guide to earning and saving thousands on the Internet / Barbara Webb
with Maureen Heck.
            p.   cm.
      Includes index.
      ISBN 0-07-145776-3
            1. Mothers—Finance, Personal.   2. Consumer education—Computer network
resources.   3. Shopping—Computer network resources.   4. Teleshopping.
5. Home economics—Computer network resources.   6. Mothers—Employment—
Computer network resources.   I. Heck, Maureen.   II. Title.

      HG179.W383   2006
      381'.142'0852—dc22   2005016740

1 2 3 4 5 6 7 8 9 0   FGR/FGR   0 9 8 7 6 5

ISBN 0-07-145776-3

McGraw-Hill books are available at special quantity discounts to use as premiums and
sales promotions, or for use in corporate training programs. For more information, please
write to the Director of Special Sales, Professional Publishing, McGraw-Hill, Two Penn
Plaza, New York, NY 10121-2298. Or contact your local bookstore.

This book is printed on acid-free paper.

This book is affectionately dedicated:

To my husband, Jamie, whose loving support makes all things possible; to my children, Cassie, Cody, and Corbin, who make motherhood a constant joy; and to my mom, Darlene, whose love and guidance prove time and time again—mothers are one of life's greatest treasures
—Barb Webb

To my husband, Eric, and daughter, Kaylee, without whose love and support none of this would be possible, as well as the rest of my family, especially my father, who has always believed in me
—Maureen Heck

Contents

Preface

Setting Up for Success: Computer and Internet Basics

The methodology and principles in this book rely on a basic understanding of the Internet. Accessing the Internet at home requires setting up your computer and finding an Internet Service Provider (ISP) you are comfortable with. The ISP will give you a window in which to connect to the Internet. To choose an ISP, we suggest that you ask your friends and family what they use and like, and check with your local providers for details about costs and services best suited to your needs.

The four most popular types of Internet connections are dial-up, cable, digital subscriber line (DSL), and satellite. Depending on which choice you make, speed of connection will vary. Dial-up will generally suffice and is an inexpensive way to get started. You may wish to inquire about high-speed Internet access later to enhance your experience.

Once you are connected and ready to see what the Internet has to offer, there are a few terms and basic operations you'll need to understand. A list of basic Internet terminology used throughout this guide are listed in the Glossary. It will be helpful to review these terms before you get started.

A primary tool and basic operation function that you'll use while surfing the Net is a search engine. A search engine is a website with extensive database software to help you find web-sites containing the information you need.

Think of your search engine as your online librarian. You access the search engine website and then type in key words about the subject you wish to locate. For example, you are planning your family vacation to Florida and want to see if there are resorts or theme parks of interest. You would first go to the search engine site and then use the index to search for "Florida Vacations" or "Florida Theme Parks." The search engine index would then return a comprehensive listing of websites that best match your needs.

Here are a few search engines to begin with:

- Alta Vista (www.altavista.com)
- Google (www.google.com)
- Excite (www.excite.com)
- Yahoo! (www.yahoo.com)

Another tool you're likely to access daily is your e-mail. Electronic mail is the main vehicle for exchanging packets of information with other users on the Net. When you sign up with your ISP, you will most likely receive an e-mail address—for example, JaneDoe@emailaddress.com.

Setting Up Your E-Mail for Success

E-mail has become the primary communication vehicle of the Internet. Perhaps you already use your e-mail to communicate with friends, family, or work associates. Your e-mail account will play a significant role in your success at using the meth-ods outlined in this book. As you delve into these opportuni-ties, it is important to set yourself up to succeed from the very beginning.

Establishing a plan for organizing and maintaining e-mail is a critical part of our methodology. The simplest and most effective way of doing this is to begin with a minimum of two e-mail accounts: one for personal mail and one for Internet use. Your personal mail will be used for correspondence with friends, family, business associates, banking, and all other areas of your personal life. You will use your Internet e-mail for your Internet activities, such as signing up for free samples or communication on a website.

We suggest that you use your ISP-provided e-mail address as your personal mail account. Many ISPs allow you to establish additional accounts. Contact your provider to find out how many additional e-mail accounts you may add, as well as how to access them. Then simply set up another account for your Internet activity.

If your ISP does not allow additional accounts, there are numerous free Internet account services that will provide you with the extra addresses you need. There are also a number of paid services offering unlimited e-mail capacity, and you may find, down the road, that they will suit your needs better.

We happen to love the free stuff, so here are some sites with which to register for free e-mail accounts:

- Yahoo (www.mail.yahoo.com)
- Excite (www.excite.com)
- MSN Hotmail (www.hotmail.com)
- GMail by Google (www.gmail.google.com)
- Lycos (www.mail.lycos.com)

One thing to note with free e-mail accounts is that you may be subject to commercial ads and occasional promotional e-mails from the provider of the account, but remember, you are never obligated to purchase or enroll in anything that will not be of benefit to you.

While establishing your Internet-use e-mail account, you'll need to think about naming conventions. To ensure privacy and protection, avoid using your real name and other personal details. We also suggest you choose something simple, so your e-mail address is easy to type and remember, keeping in mind that common names and terms are usually taken.

After gaining a basic understanding of Internet terms and tools, and establishing your secondary e-mail account, you are ready to learn the tips and tricks designed to make you a bargain-hunting, money-saving, and dollar-savvy Internet mom!

Acknowledgments

O ur deepest gratitude to our agent, Caren Johnson, of the Peter Rubie Literary Agency; our editor, Michele Matrisciani; and everyone at McGraw-Hill for believing in us. Special thanks also to Meg Leder for her faith in us and to Maryann Layton for providing the Internet home that nurtured our friendship.

Introduction

Not Just a Book—a Way of Life

Each day, we don our fuzzy bunny slippers, make the kids breakfast, and begin earning money, savings, and rewards without ever having to change out of our pajamas. What could be better?

Our journey began as a quest to simplify our lives, supplement our incomes, and enrich our daily routines. The quest developed into a rewarding lifestyle perfected over a three-year period, all within the comforts of our own homes. Our combination of retail, marketing, communications, and technology backgrounds made it possible for us to discover and develop the best ways to tap into a wealth of Internet resources, incorporating them into an easy-to-follow guide anyone can use.

You do not have to be a Net professional to benefit from our methods. All you need is a PC, this book, and the desire to improve your life.

By sharing this information, we hope to empower other moms across the country to reap the rich rewards of what we have dubbed the MOM(dot)COM lifestyle. We intend to simplify your life by teaching you how to shop, save, and earn money, all on your home computer, leaving you more time for your family and personal passions. We'd love for you to tap into the "hidden" gems of the Internet because more moms using the Internet means more deals, more coupons, more surveys, and lots more fun for everyone. We want you to use our insider information to line your pockets and enhance your life. We are moms, too, and we know how hard it can be to make ends meet. Once we realized the true benefits provided by the Internet, there was no way we could keep this secret to ourselves; we wanted other moms to benefit just as we do. In the pages ahead, you will learn to triple your savings on shopping sprees, trade and sell unwanted items for cold hard cash, get paid for your opinion, learn the ins and outs of mystery shopping, and much more.

How far this book will take you is up to you. Once you have the know-how, the sky really is the limit.

Viewing the numbers clearly brings home the full value of using our methods. How would you like to earn up to $500 a month or more, and save thousands a year? Multiplied out over a year's time, you could see more than $16,000 in income and savings combined! It can be done. We've done it; now let us show you how. It's so easy, because you choose what methods and when to use the principles supplied in this book. Are you a night owl? No problem. Shop your favorite department store at 3:00 A.M. Are your kids in bed by 7:00 P.M.? Sit down and do a few paid surveys. The Internet is never closed, and it is ready and waiting for you to tap into its secrets.

Our methodology is not a get-rich-quick scheme. Our step-by-step guide contains honest and proven ways to earn extra income and savings for your family by tapping into the secrets of the World Wide Web (WWW). The bulk of the information contained in this book cannot be found on the Internet. We have spent many hours searching, testing, and perfecting our methods so you don't have to. The key is knowing where to look for opportunities and what to do with them when you find them.

This guide has been divided into two easy-to-follow sections that will have you on your way to success in no time. In Part 1, we take an in-depth look at all of the opportunities presented on the Internet, such as couponing, comparative shopping, selling, trading, mystery shopping, and paid surveys. In Part 2, we show you how to put it all together and make it work in your daily life, with sections covering hot topics such as travel, entertainment, goods and services for your home, your baby, toddlers, and teens. Included in each chapter is an array of time-saving tips, smart ways to stay safe and avoid pitfalls such as spam and scams, original ideas for integrating each topic into your daily life, hundreds of links and resources, and practical advice you won't find elsewhere.

In addition, we at MOM(dot)COM (www.momdotcom .net) have established a 100 percent free, ad-free, gimmick-free website for our readers and the Internet community. It contains supplemental materials such as sample forms, reference guides, new links, and even a newsletter. Our monthly newsletter offers subscribers seasonal freebies, deal information, our recipe of the month, author updates, contests, promotions, and all kinds of goodies! You also will find weekly listings of free samples and hot offers, along with special printables and promotions. There's always something new happening at MOM(dot)COM. You can feel 100 percent secure that we will not share your e-mail or private information with any outside parties.

We live this lifestyle and garner the benefits every day. We have earned money doing surveys, saved thousands at the grocery store, and developed a lifelong friendship—all by implementing the principles you'll read in this book. You can, too. Let's get started!

Part 1

Find a World
of Savings
and Earn Money
on the Web

Chapter 1
Free Stuff

Freebie ('frE-bE): the something for nothing that
everyone wants

*I really wanted to try this new fabric softener, but I
couldn't justify the six-dollar-plus price tag. Then I
received a free sample and coupon in the mail and have
been hooked ever since. I never would've purchased this
without trying it first. I'm thrilled, and my clothes have
never smelled better.*

—Lydia, *Florida*

What Kind of Free Stuff?

We're not certain who first said "the best things in life are free,"
but they were definitely on to something. While we doubt they
were talking about a free sample of hot sauce, they were still
on the right track. How would you like to find your mailbox

full of free samples, coupons, and exciting products instead of just finding bills? Free stuff, commonly referred to as freebies, is abundant on the Internet. In this chapter, we will show you how to tap into this parcel treasure. While your mail carriers may mumble expletives under their breath when delivering your mail, you will be joyfully anticipating its arrival each day.

Let's begin by exploring the different types of freebies available to Internet consumers:

- **100 percent free products.** Items are completely free with no strings attached.
- **Almost free.** These offers may require you to send your request via snail mail (the United States Postal Service) and to include a self-addressed stamped envelope (SASE) for return mail, or to pay a small shipping and handling fee to try the product. The Almost-free category also includes mail-in offers for free items that may require proof of purchase or universal product codes (UPCs) taken directly off the purchased product.
- **1-800 freebies.** This category includes freebies that can be obtained by calling an 800 number and speaking with a live operator or navigating through an automated system. Generally these items are also 100 percent free and do not require a purchase or commitment.
- **Free printables.** This category refers to materials you may access on the Internet for free and print them out using your personal computer printer. Free printables on the Web include, but are not limited to, scrapbook pages, coloring book pages and activity sheets, calendars, bookmarks, charts and logs, greeting cards, teaching materials, coupons and rebates, shopping lists and checklists, and gift tags.
- **Free services.** This category refers to nontangible items and products, such as free e-mail accounts, software, website hosting, and even free Internet access.

How Do I Find the Free Stuff?

Finding free stuff on the Internet is easier than you might think. There are two basic ways to go about getting free items and services. The first (easy) way is finding them yourself. The second (easier) way is letting others find them for you. For the sake of expediency in getting you started on the path to freebies, we'll begin by exploring the second option first.

There are several methods for gaining access to other people's freebie finds on the Internet. Let's explore the two top methods of free sample clubs and freebie websites.

Free Sample Clubs

Free sample clubs work with national vendors to offer samples, coupons, products, services, and other items of interest to targeted groups. They achieve this by having a subscriber base, namely you.

These clubs typically require completion of a simple registration process involving selecting a user name and providing a little information about your family and interests. This information allows them to tailor their promotions to you. For example, if you own a cat, you may qualify for free cat food samples. If you do not own a cat, you would be unlikely to receive such offers.

Some clubs require you to visit the site daily to find out what free promotions are offered, others will send you a direct mailing via e-mail, and still others will send you samples and coupons automatically through the mail based on the preferences you indicated.

To get you started, we've listed a few clubs:

- StartSampling (www.startsampling.com)
- EverSave (www.eversave.com)
- Home Made Simple (www.homemadesimple.com)

- Club Olay (www.olay.com)
- Quality Health (www.qualityhealth.com)

The most important thing to remember is to read through the club's website information to learn what is expected of you as a member.

Freebie Websites

There are numerous websites across the Internet dedicated solely to the pursuit of freebies. Some of these sites are fabulous collections of information and offers, and other sites are merely set up as gimmicks to entice you into spending money with their sponsors. Occasionally you'll run into websites that are a combination of the two. The sites you want are those that exist with the intention of providing you with 100 percent free offers and information.

Some freebie websites to get you started are:

- MOM(dot)COM (www.momdotcom.net)
- The Frugal Shopper (www.thefrugalshopper.com)
- MyCoupons (www.mycoupons.com)
- Just Free Stuff (www.justfreestuff.com)

These websites will get you started, but you are bound to encounter many others that will help support your freebie habits.

Another fun and exciting part of Internet freebies is contests and giveaways. Most freebie websites have a designated spot for Internet contests. Be sure to check out these websites, because you can't win it if you're not in it.

The following are the most common types of contests:

■ **First 1,000 offers.** Some websites offer their freebies to a select number of participants, for example, the first 1,000 to log on to a website will get a free bottle of lotion or perfume.

These freebies are more like giveaways and have set times and dates for entry submissions. You have to be quick if you want to grab one of these offers; they go superfast.

■ **Freebies with a contest entry.** Many times signing up for a free sample will earn you an entry in a contest or sweepstakes, or vice versa. Trying that free sample of toothpaste may just win you a dream vacation to Hawaii.

■ **Sweepstakes.** Standard types of sweepstakes offer you the opportunity to win a wide variety of cash or prizes. Prizes range from home entertainment units to cash to home makeovers or vacations. The entries are free, and you never know, you could be a lucky winner.

You may encounter several time frames for sweepstakes offers: daily, weekly, monthly, and one-time only. All contests have their own rules and guidelines that must be followed in order for your entry to be counted, so be sure to read through them for a full understanding of the regulations. Some of the popular types of contest styles include essay contests, trivia contests, games, children's sweepstakes, and instant-win games.

Be aware that many contest sponsors share your mailing information with their partner companies or subsidiaries, which may cause an increase in spam or junk mail. Make sure to use your alternate e-mail account when registering for contests and watch for an opt-out checkbox typically found at the bottom of a contest entry form. This option allows you to let the company that is sponsoring the contest know that you are not interested in sharing your information with anyone other than that company.

Wait, There's More!

Another method of having others find freebies for you is by subscribing to company or freebie website mailing lists or "e-zines." Mailing lists may be distributed via e-mail or snail mail.

As with contests, the negative side to Internet mailing lists or e-zines is the increase in spam you may receive as a result of companies sharing your e-mail address with their partners or parent companies. Anytime you give your address to anyone, you run the risk of increased spam, but if the benefits outweigh the negatives for you, you may want to give them a chance. Spam, and how to reduce your risk of receiving unwanted mail, is discussed further in Chapter 12.

The same principle holds true of snail mail lists. You may see an increase in junk mail arriving in your mailbox. There are definitely more positives associated with high-quality mailing lists. If you decide to join a snail mail list, you may randomly receive samples or coupons as a perk for joining. When you join freebie website mailing lists, you will be among the first to be notified of new freebies and promotions as they become available. Often these e-zines and mailings contain helpful information like recipes, tips, rebate offers, sweepstakes, and information on other useful websites.

Some websites offering freebie-friendly e-zines or snail mail newsletters are:

- Kraft Foods (www.kraftfoods.com/kf). This website offers mom-friendly recipes, tips, and promotions, as well as the opportunity to sign up for an e-zine and a snail mail magazine.
- Nestle (www.nestleusa.com). This website offers promotions and product information for the Nestle family of products. In addition, there are links to a variety of other e-zine and snail mail newsletters.
- Woman's Day (www.womansday.com). The main website for *Woman's Day* magazine offers an option to subscribe to their e-zine containing information on related clubs, events, recipes, contests, promotions, tips, and more.

To find freebies on your own, the easiest route is to use your search engine. Begin by typing the keywords most likely to supply the best results into your favorite search engine and then browse the choices until you have found what appeals to you. For example, if your cousin is having a wedding in six months, you may want to look at wedding invitations without the hassle of having to go to a specialty store. Try typing "free sample wedding invitations" into the search engine of your choice. This should give you a nice match of results and a solid place to start.

The same practice will apply to virtually any freebie you seek, be it fabric softener, financial planning, or foundation. Now that you have a head start, log on to the Internet and grab your freebies today!

Chapter 2
Bargains

Bargain ('bär-gun): goods or services offered at out-standing prices

Two pairs of name-brand sneakers for $30 shipped. You can't beat that deal with a stick!

—Donna, *Ohio*

What a Bargain!

Bargains abound within the online community, proving that online shopping is not without merit. Imagine shopping without the crowds, bad parking, or headaches that generally accompany those excursions. Virtually anything that can be obtained in a brick-and-mortar retail store can be obtained online—and often for less. Many online retailers offer discount incentives to entice you to shop with them. Some of these discounts are easy to find and others are slightly more elusive.

How can you find the steals and deals on the Internet? Let's take a look at the complete ins and outs of online shopping beginning with comparative shopping.

Comparison Shopping

An important aspect of finding Internet deals is to know your prices before you shop. Before shopping online, look through retailers' fliers and familiarize yourself with regular and sale prices in stores. Many retailers are taking advantage of the exposure the World Wide Web provides, and you may be surprised to find out that prices vary dramatically from site to site. How can you figure out which site offers the best deal? Easy! There are websites that provide the comparisons for you. Not only do they offer price comparisons, but many also offer written product reviews and other retailers' ratings and reviews of the online store. Here are some comparison sites for you to test:

- Epinions (www.epinions.com)
- Bizrate (www.bizrate.com)
- Pricescan (www.pricescan.com)
- Froogle (www.froogle.com)

Comparison shopping sites are quite simple to navigate, and how you do so depends on the shopping you are doing. For example, you need a new vacuum but do not have a specific model in mind. If you head over to a comparison website such as Epinions, and enter the word "vacuums" into its search feature, this will yield a return of all vacuums supported on their site—everything from canister models to uprights. If you know you would like a bagless upright, you can narrow the search by adding the keywords "upright" and "bagless" to your initial search. Now you will only see vacuums meeting these criteria, thereby making it easier to determine what your choices are. If you do happen to have a specific model in mind, entering the complete name of the product or the model number into the search feature will yield results for that specific item.

After narrowing your choices down to the items or type of product you are most interested in, you will then be able to see pricing, read customer reviews, and check out the retailers that offer that product.

More Savings!

I saved an extra 20 percent and got free shipping on the flowers I sent my mom for Mother's Day. Without that code, I'm not sure I would've been able to surprise her this year.

—LAURIE, *Nevada*

Now that you have found the best online deal for your purchases, it can't possibly get any better—or can it? It just might with the aid of supersecret online codes. Okay, they are not really "supersecret," but the majority of online shoppers do not know they exist and are spending extra money unnecessarily. You will find codes offering a variety of savings, such as free shipping, a set percentage or dollar amount off your order, or even free items with your purchase. Imagine buying two pairs of jeans and getting the sweater you wanted for free. It's often possible with the use of online codes. Online codes are added savings that can be applied to your order at the time of checkout. Some sites have their codes readily available and others require you to do a little digging to see what opportunities await you.

There are two types of coupon codes that circulate the Internet regularly:

■ **One-time-use codes.** These codes are intended to be used one time by one consumer. They are usually offered directly to you from the retailer in hopes of gaining you as a loyal customer.

■ **Multiple-use codes.** These codes can be used over and over by many online users.

There are several ways these codes reach consumers via the Internet:

■ **Direct e-mail.** Remember that e-zine you signed up for? These types of e-mails frequently contain codes for a percentage or dollar amount off your next purchase.

■ **Online code sites.** An ever-evolving area of the Internet consists of online code websites. These sites generally offer an extensive list of coupon codes for a variety of online retailers. Here are some code websites to check:

- Naughty Codes (www.naughtycodes.com)
- Slick Deals (www.slickdeals.net)
- Able Shoppers (www.ableshoppers.com)
- Jump on Deals (www.jumpondeals.com)
- Edeals Etc. (www.edealsetc.com)

■ **Direct referrals.** Some online retailers may offer you the ability to solicit business for them by providing you with a code to e-mail to your friends and family. This is a win-win situation for everyone involved, as the company gains new customers and your friends and family save money. Usually you will be offered an incentive for circulating these codes, such as additional savings on future products from the retailer.

■ **Online deal sites.** These forum boards often have sections dedicated specifically to online coupon codes as well as online deals. Be sure to check here, and do not hesitate to ask if anyone is aware of any codes for a specific store, these community members are often extremely helpful. You'll find more information on forums in Chapter 10, "Peer Networking." You can begin with these deal sites:

- Fat Wallet (www.fatwallet.com)
- Crazy Cool Dealz (www.crazycooldealz.com)
- Deal Catcher (www.dealcatcher.com)

■ **Retailer websites.** Many of the larger retailers will display their codes prominently on their websites. Sometimes they will be displayed on the home page, and other times you may have to dig around the site a little to find them. Look for areas of the website labeled "Today's Deals" or something similar to see if the retailer offers any codes or additional savings for shopping its online store.

Cracking the Codes

Here are a few additional tips to ensure your successful use of Internet coupon codes:

■ **Check expirations.** Codes will generally be accompanied by an expiration date or may come with other restrictions. Be sure you fully understand the requirements for using the coupon code you have found, and make sure the code is valid before you attempt to use it.

■ **Using coupon codes.** Once you have found a valid coupon code and are ready to apply it to your order, there will generally be a clear spot in which to enter the code number or code information. For example, you may have found the code SUMMERSAVINGS, which offers free shipping on orders of $25 or more. At checkout, look for a spot to enter promotional codes or gift certificates; enter your coupon code here.

■ **Double-check your order.** Before you complete your online purchase, scan through the billing details and check to see whether the code took off the appropriate dollar amount, applied free shipping, or whatever else was offered in the promotion. If you slip up, finish the transaction, and forget to apply a code, never hesitate to contact the company to see if you can still receive the discount.

Brick-and-Mortar Bargains

Before you head out to your local retailer to shop, be sure to prepare yourself just as you would for Internet comparison shopping and consider completing these additional steps:

■ Check print circulars for sales.

■ Scan the Internet for product information.

■ Visit the price comparison websites and print off copies of your search findings to take with you to the retailer. Some B&M retailers will price match Internet prices, and you'll save the cost of shipping. In addition, you'll have an excellent guide to help determine if you are getting a good deal on the product you select.

■ Look on the Internet for printable coupons for savings at the retailers you'll be visiting. Also check your mail, newspapers, and magazines for special offers. Two websites to check are Coupon Maker (www.couponmaker.com) and Valpack (www.valpack.com).

■ Write a list. Impulse buying is a financial killer. Write a list of your needs before you leave and bring it with you. You'll have better focus when shopping and will be less tempted to wander around the store picking up items you weren't planning on purchasing.

The previous suggestions are also discussed in greater length throughout in the following chapters.

After mentally and physically preparing yourself for your retail shopping excursion, the next powerful weapon in the arsenal of the savvy shopper is to understand store clearance and sale cycles. Knowing how stores typically regulate their merchandise will allow you to shop at the best time possible to grab the lowest price on the items you need.

Retailers follow various clearance and sale patterns to clear their stores of excess or seasonal products and make room for the new products coming in. The key is to understand some of the methodology behind the cycles.

First, many products are seasonal and for that reason will immediately go on sale when the season ends. For example, the very best time to buy Christmas items is in January or February, as you will find them for a fraction of the price they sold at during the months of November and December.

There are two core areas of seasonal bargains for us to explore—holiday and common items. Let's take a look at the cycles for each.

Holiday Items

Begin now to purchase your holiday items a year in advance, if possible. You will save hundreds of dollars over the course of the year. Simply store them in easily accessible containers and pull them out when the holiday arrives.

Typically most retailers discount holiday items by 50 percent or more the day after the holiday. The few days after a holiday are the best times to pick up the items you really had your eye on but couldn't bring yourself to pay full price for. Hold out a few more days or a week or two longer, and the holiday items will be at even steeper discounts of 60 to 90 percent off. The selection will be trimmer, but it's a great time to pick up the smaller items, such as wrapping paper or Easter grass. It's also a little known fact that some perishables, such as chocolate and cocoa, can be stored at a cool temperature for a year with little to no effect. You may want to scan the Internet for some frugal mom websites to learn more about the ins and outs of food storage. Also be sure to check the United States Department of Agriculture (USDA) Food Safety and Inspection Service website (www.fsis.usda.gov) for the latest information on proper food storage and safety.

It may feel odd at first to pick up these items a year ahead of time, but when a holiday rolls around, you will be relieved to have your shopping done and supplies on hand. Not to mention, you'll have racked up a massive amount of savings and extended your dollar power.

Common Items

We've prepared a special calendar to give you a guide to the best times of year to shop for particular items that you need or have on your list for gifts. It is good practice at the beginning of each year to decide who you need to purchase gifts for that year. Consider what types of items you might want to purchase and plan your shopping months accordingly. This will stretch your buying power more than you can imagine since you can be on the look out for deals ahead of time.

Please note that although we've assigned some items to December, it is the worst time of year to go shopping for two reasons. One, retailers are pulling out all the stops to get you to increase your spending, not to save your dollars. Two, as we all know, the stores are crowded and the availability of popular items is lessened, which doesn't allow for maximum stockup shopping when needed or for being able to get the items you want. You may find yourself having to buy a more expensive item or a replacement product to compensate, which will not aid you in achieving your savings goals.

Table 2.1 shows the special buying calendar to guide you through each month of the year. Keep in mind that this is merely a guide to monthly deals. If you see a bargain on a product not listed for a certain month, by all means, grab it!

Additional Bargain Hunting Tips

While you are searching for bargains, keep in mind the following:

- **Don't forget eBay.** Online auction sites are a great place to find amazing deals on items that your family may need. You can often find brand-new, never-used merchandise being auctioned for rock-bottom prices. Many online auctioneers will offer additional savings to buyers that take advantage of their "Buy It Now" feature by offering a bonus such as free shipping or a free item. Flip to Chapter 8 for an insider look at auctions.
- **Always check for a code.** Do not make the mistake of assuming that smaller online retailers do not offer incentives to bring potential shoppers to their site. At a minimum, do a quick search of your favorite coupon code sites and see what they turn up; you may be pleasantly surprised.
- **Check your favorite retailer's clearance rack.** Even online stores have clearance sections. You will find merchandise reduced in a similar way to that of brick-and-mortar stores. Look for clearance items throughout the season for some of your best bargains.
- **If you have to pass up a deal—pass it on.** You found a pair of jeans for $10, with free shipping, and an additional 20 percent off at checkout. The problem is they only come in size eight and you're a size twelve. The deal may not work for you, but it may come in handy for someone else. What about your daughter or niece? You may want to consider buying them as a gift. What about your best friend who is a size eight or your online friends? E-mail them or share the information on an online website.
- **Check your deal sites often.** Many times these deals are on a first-come, first-served basis. When a website's supply is depleted, the sale is what the online community refers

TABLE 2.1 DEALS-BY-MONTH SHOPPING GUIDE

Month	Grocery	Fashion	Other	Seasonal
January	Holiday food Clearance items Baking goods Frozen foods Diet-related foods	Shoes Winter jackets Winter accessories Costume jewelry Athletic shoes Athletic wear	Calendars Linen Towels Appliances Toys White sales	After Christmas, Hanukah, Kwanzaa, and New Year's clearances
February	Candy Lobster Steak	Lingerie Menswear Jewelry Picture frames	Curtains Electronics Sports equipment	After Valentine's Day clearance
March	Frozen foods	Ice skates Infant/Children's clothing	Carpet China Ski equipment Luggage	After St. Patrick's Day clearance
April	Ham Eggs	Socks and hosiery Women's shoes Dresses Suits	Garden tools Office furniture	After Easter clearance
May	Condiments	Handbags Sleep/loungewear Jewelry Sportswear Spring outerwear	Kitchenware Rugs Tires Baskets	After Mother's Day clearance

Month				
June	Dairy products	Menswear Wallets	Hardware Electronics Sports equipment	After Father's Day clearance
July	Fish Corn Watermelon Barbeque items	Summer clothing Athletic shoes Sunglasses Watches	Paint Fuel Building materials	After July Fourth clearance
August	Canned goods	Fall outerwear Silver jewelry	Patio furniture Summer sports equipment Cosmetics Air conditioners White sales Office supplies	Back-to-school specials
September		Bathing suits Fall fashions	Fall flower bulbs Bicycles Lamps	Back-to-school clearance
October	Pumpkins Squash	Storewide clearances Jeans	Blankets Toys Home health care items Fishing supplies Appliances	
November	Baking products Holiday season items Turkey and ham	Suits	Small appliances Hunting supplies	Halloween clearance
December	Holiday season items Turkey and ham	Winter clothing Watches	Furniture Appliances Automobiles	Thanksgiving clearance After Christmas clearance

to as "dead." By keeping up with your favorite sites, you stand a greater chance of being able to take advantage of the deals presented daily.

■ **Don't miss a markdown.** Did you ever purchase an item one week just to find that it went on sale the next week for less than you paid? Find out what the retailer's price reduction policy is. Many of them will be happy to refund you the difference or allow you to return and rebuy the merchandise at a lower cost. This works equally well in both online and neighborhood stores.

Whatever elements of bargain hunting you decide to use, remember to have fun and enjoy the thrill of getting the best deal!

Chapter 3
Point Programs

Point ('point): a unit of measurement used to earn extras

I spend hundreds online around Christmastime to save me the hassle of crowded malls. I couldn't believe it when I found out I can get free gifts and dollars back too. It's like getting a Christmas present of my own—just for shopping!

—CLAIRE, *Michigan*

What's the Point of All These Points?

The Internet already provides us with wonderful options: online shopping, fast access to businesses, and a wealth of information. Now to make a good thing even better, point programs have cropped up to enhance your Internet usage. These programs add extra incentives for spending your time and dollars on the Internet. They allow you to earn dollars back and other rewards for shopping specific retailers or spending time reading through offers. Some of the point companies even reward you for shopping offline as well.

Would you like to take advantage of these enticing programs? Let's begin by exploring how point programs work and the best ways for you to maximize your savings. Most point programs are simple to understand, and the rewards are easily calculated. There are three main point categories:

- **Purchase-related points.** Some programs give a set number of points for purchasing items from a vendor who participates in the program. For example, you spend $40 to send flowers through an online florist to your mom for her birthday. If the particular point program you are enrolled with offers 5 points per dollar spent with the online florist, after completing your sale you'd be rewarded with 200 points.

- **Credit card points.** Some point programs give you points based on your credit card usage. The credit card may be particular to the point program, or you may be able to enroll all of your credit cards. Points are typically earned by dollars charged. For example, your monthly credit card purchases add up to $426 and your point program offers 3 points per dollar spent per month. You would earn 1,278 points for the month.

- **Activity-related points.** Some programs offer points for completion of offers, visiting websites, completing surveys, or other activities. The offers may be contingent on signing up for a service, club, or promotional item. For example, your program may offer you 5 points to visit a vendor's website to read through a promotion, such as a book club offer. If you choose to sign up for the offer, the point program offers 200 extra points, thereby giving you a total of 205 points.

Many programs will combine these three options or offer additional opportunities as well.

Where Do I Find Point Programs?

Now that you understand the point basics, where do you begin to find the best programs? We'll help get you started:

- MyPoints (www.mypoints.com)
- Club Mom (www.clubmom.com)
- Ebates (www.ebates.com)
- UPromise (www.upromise.com)
- Milesource (www.milesource.com)

You will find additional point programs available for you to take advantage of as well. Here are a few ways to find additional programs:

- Use your preferred search engine to run a search for "point programs."
- Ask your friends, family, and online friends what programs they participate in or have knowledge of.
- Ask your local retailers if they have programs or if they participate in any national programs.
- Find out if your favorite forum board has established shopping links.

Making More Points

In order to maximize your earnings with point programs, use the following suggestions when appropriate.

Remember to Use Your Point Programs

While with some programs, points may be calculated automatically through the use of a credit card, many programs require the use of specific links or that you follow certain steps to collect your points. It's often easy to forget to go through your point programs while you are shopping and in the process, you will miss out on the extra savings. Here are a few ideas to help you remember to use your programs:

■ Designate a specific credit card for online use and tape the point program website information to the back of the card. That way each time you pick it up, you'll have a reminder. Also, using one card for Internet use is a safe practice and allows you to easily notice if your card number is ever compromised.

■ Use a sticky note or tape a reminder to your computer reminding you to use your favorite point program websites when shopping.

■ If you know you will actively be participating in online shopping on a particular day, open your point program websites first and use the links for your shopping quest.

Keep Track of Your Efforts

It may seem like an unnecessary step, but it's often a good idea to record your point earnings. Keep them in a separate spreadsheet on your computer or in a hard-copy ledger. Record the date, the store, your purchase amount or a short description of the offer, points earned, and the point program you used. Often the vendors are responsible for communicating your information back to the point program, and occasionally you may not receive credit for an offer. If you've kept a log, it makes it easy to contact the point program customer service staff to obtain credit for your actions. Most programs offer a detailed breakdown of your points and how they were accumulated, so it is very simple to check for discrepancies.

Remember to Cash In

Be sure to watch for expiration dates and cash your points in for monetary rewards or the items offered. Some programs require that you redeem your points within a limited time period or they expire. If you are participating in such a program, write yourself a reminder on your calendar to check your sites near point expiration dates, or get into the habit of checking the websites weekly or monthly to be certain that you are taking full advantage of your rewards.

Use an Alternate E-Mail Account

Consider setting up a separate e-mail account for your point programs so that you can always stay on top of current information and promotions. Remember some programs give you points simply for reading your e-mails and you don't want to miss out on the easy points.

Consider Storing Your Points

Check the point level opportunities with your program. Some programs offer bigger and better items at higher point levels, meaning the more you accumulate, the better the reward you may receive. Don't be tempted to grab for a small reward when you could save your points an extra month or two to get a much larger reward. It may be worth the wait!

Spread the News

Share the information with your friends. Many point programs offer you extra points for referring friends and family. If you like the point program, then share the wealth and gain and reap the rewards of your kindness.

Maximize Your Points

If you belong to several point programs, be sure to take a moment to find out which one offers the best point match for the particular shop from which you are making your purchase or for a particular offer you've been considering. Also find out if you can use more than one point program to double your earnings. For example, if you have a credit card that accumulates points, you can use it and still go through another point program website link to earn points with both programs.

Point Program Pitfalls

Occasionally you will run across a point program that, while well meaning, may not prove beneficial to you. You may also find a fabulous point program that occasionally chooses to send through a questionable offer. These are some of the more popular pitfalls to steer clear of:

- **Enrollment fees.** Be wary of point programs that require an enrollment fee. You should investigate and fully understand the terms of the offer before signing up. After all, the purpose of a point program is to earn money or special items, not to spend more money to get them.
- **Shipping fees.** Watch out for programs that charge shipping fees. Shipping and handling should be included when you redeem your points for cash or prizes. Again, the purpose of a point program is to earn free items, not to have to spend additional money to get your rewards.
- **Too-good-to-be-true offers.** Occasionally, you will encounter a point program that offers you the potential to earn high dollar rewards or hundreds and thousands in cash with very little effort. The reality is legitimate point programs reward you realistically for your efforts and spending habits. If you are spending less than $100 a month shopping through their links, it would not be very prudent of them to offer you a $1,000 reward in return.
- **E-mail point programs.** There are several genuine point programs that incorporate surveys and points for read-

■ **Shipping fees.** Watch out for programs that charge shipping fees. Shipping and handling should be included when you redeem your points for cash or prizes. Again, the purpose of a point program is to earn free items, not to have to spend additional money to get your rewards.

■ **Too-good-to-be-true offers.** Occasionally, you will encounter a point program that offers you the potential to earn high dollar rewards or hundreds and thousands in cash with very little effort. The reality is legitimate point programs reward you realistically for your efforts and spending habits. If you are spending less than $100 a month shopping through their links, it would not be very prudent of them to offer you a $1,000 reward in return.

■ **E-mail point programs.** There are several genuine point programs that incorporate surveys and points for reading e-mails, so do not discount this option. Instead, be on the lookout for programs that offer you hundreds of dollars in rewards or specific dollar amounts for reading your e-mail. Often they have unachievable cash-out levels and basically all you will be doing is inviting spam into your e-mail account.

■ **Enrolling in credit card point programs.** Credit card–based point programs can be very lucrative if you tend to pay your bills in full each month or carry a low monthly balance. If you normally carry high balances or plan to only make the minimum payments each month, be sure to check the terms of the credit card before signing up for the point program. Often these cards have a finance rate between 19 and 28 percent (and sometimes higher) attached. You will wind up paying more in interest fees than you will redeem for cash or prizes through the point program. In essence, you may be better off in the long run purchasing a product outright rather than participating with a high-interest-rate credit card to earn the points to get the prize for "free."

Point programs can be very lucrative, easy to participate in, and enjoyable. By learning to maximize your points and avoid unnecessary pitfalls, you'll be well on your way to earning great prizes, discounts, and cash rewards!

Chapter 4

Coupon-Related Savings

Couponing ('kü- pän (ng)) the intelligent art of clipping your way to savings

Buying formula, baby food, and diapers for our twin daughters nearly wiped out our family savings. What a blessing when I learned how to combine coupons, rebates, and sales cycles. We were able to cut our weekly grocery bill almost in half!

—KAREN, *Illinois*

Everyday Savings

What if every time you went to the grocery store, the cashier gave you a free bag of groceries to take home with your purchase? How about if you went shopping for a pair of jeans and brought home a matching shirt for free? Does this sound too good to be true? It's not. Manufacturers and retail chains around the country are vying for your business. So much so that they are willing to let you obtain their products at a discounted rate or even for free in order to get your attention or reward your loyalty to their brand. They offer premium incentives in the form of coupons, rebates, mail-in offers, sales, and various other promotions.

Before we delve into how to use these different programs to your advantage, let us take a quick look at each type individually:

- **Coupons.** By far the most easily recognized and readily available incentives from companies are coupons. Coupons are generally found in various paper formats from online printable versions to the standard flyers included in newspapers.
- **Rebates.** Often overlooked by the average consumer, product rebates can add up to huge savings over time. Not always easy to find, rebates are generally offered as either "instant redemption," meaning the discounted amount is taken off the product or service at the time of sale, or "after-sale redemption," meaning the rebate is obtained electronically or by mail after the product has been purchased.
- **Mail-in offers.** This type of incentive usually requires you to purchase products first, and then mail in or electronically submit the required information and/or forms to receive additional products, coupons, gift certificates, or other promotional items.
- **Sales.** In a fairly elaborate process, retailers work with manufacturers to promote and increase purchases of their product through weekly, monthly, or yearly in-store or online sales. Many of these sales are advertised via flyers in newspapers or direct mailings to consumers.
- **Other forms of promotion.** This category encompasses the random promotions that crop up from time to time, such as in-store samplings and coupon giveaways, or redemption of a product for an unrelated service discount, such as

bringing an empty can of soda to obtain a dollar amount off admission to a local theme park.

Now that we are comfortable with the various forms of incentives, we will explore the nooks and crannies of each to find out how to make them work best and give us maximum savings.

Coupons: Don't Leave Home Without Them

The most popular form of incentive offered by manufacturers and retailers today is coupons. Three of the most common places to find money-saving coupons are the Internet, Sunday newspaper circulars, and direct mailings from manufacturers.

Have you used coupons before? Are you an experienced coupon clipper? Or does the whole idea seem a little daunting to you? Regardless of what your couponing experience is, you will find this section to be an excellent and invaluable guide to saving the maximum amount possible on each and every shopping excursion.

As we begin our couponing journey, let's talk about the variety of sources providing these precious paper savings.

- **Print media.** Local newspapers are a rich source for finding coupons. Look in the main circular inserts, especially in the Sunday edition. It's always a good idea to flip through the newspaper pages as well, often there will be coupon advertisements printed directly on news pages. Some newspapers also offer special supplements that contain advertisements with coupons included. In addition to the newspaper, you will find coupons in various magazines and occasionally even in books. Don't leave any page unflipped in your quest for coupons.
- **Internet.** A growing number of companies are using the Internet as a vehicle to provide coupons to consumers.

Some of these coupons are printable and redeemable in retail stores, and others are electronic and can only be used with online purchases. Be sure to check your favorite grocery store's website for printable coupon savings; many times they will offer penny items or other high-value coupons as an incentive to shop at their store.

■ **Manufacturers.** Do you like a particular product? Then call or e-mail the manufacturer directly. Let them know whether you are a loyal fan or are just simply interested in giving their products a try, and ask if they have any coupons available. It is definitely worth a few minutes of your time. Many manufacturers will send a generous supply of coupons and sometimes other fun items and offers too. The key here is to be sincere in your praise and your request. Companies love to reward loyal or potential customers.

■ **Direct mail.** Wait, stop—don't throw that piece of mail away without opening it. There may be a valuable coupon inside. More and more, manufacturers are competing through the mail to get your attention. What you may think is just a piece of junk mail could be an envelope or postcard containing a high-value coupon or even coupons for free items.

■ **Point of purchase.** Manufacturers often provide supermarkets with coupons to place near their products right on the shelves. Keep an eye out for these, as they are often high value and there is no limit to the number you can take. In the coupon world, these are referred to as "blinkies" as the coupon holder often has a light that blinks to attract attention when sensing a consumer is near.

■ **Other.** Coupons sometimes pop up in interesting places. Check the backs of all your receipts for future savings, and ask store personnel if there is a designated space for coupons or if they have any special packets to give away with purchases. Watch for coupon-sharing "baskets" that may be located in your local library, health club, or other local facilities. Many organizations have established a receptacle of some sort in which you can drop off unneeded coupons for someone else to use. Another often-overlooked place to obtain coupons (and samples) is your doctor's office. Formula and pharmaceutical companies generously donate coupons and product samples to clinics and hospitals in order to obtain their endorsement and to reach an audience (you) that may be interested in their products. Check with your local recycling center to see if you can pick up some extra Sunday circulars from them. Get your family members and friends involved in hunting for coupons and swap coupons with your online friends.

Coupons are all around us, so keep your mind and your eyes open to the possibilities and you will find a multitude of resources to add to your savings.

I Have All These Coupons, Now What Do I Do with Them?

The next step to being successful in the couponing game is to formulate an organizational strategy that suits your individual style and needs. Keeping your coupons in order will help ensure that you never miss an opportunity to increase your savings. While there are many different ways to organize, here are some of the more popular and proven methods to help get you started:

- **Coupon holders.** These handy little files are capable of fitting in an average-size purse and are available through multiple venues, including office supply stores and general retailers. Basically, they are miniversions of the expanding files commonly used in offices. The holder has various sections in which to store and organize your coupons. Each section can be labeled to allow you to easily identify the section of coupons.

■ **Photo albums.** Some couponers use small photo albums to organize their coupons for store use. This method allows you to easily flip through the pages and see what coupons you have available. The user generally divides the coupons into sections such as Food, Beverages, and Baby for easy reference. You may also consider having separate albums for separate needs. For example, one album would serve as a holder for grocery store coupons and another would be used for retail and restaurant coupons.

■ **File boxes.** Some coupon users find that a small file box suits their needs best. Similar to recipe boxes, file boxes can be found at most office supply stores and other retail outlets. Two advantages to using a file box over a coupon holder are the extra space and the ability to label main categories and subcategories. For example, instead of just having the general label of Beverages, you could add labels for Milk, Coffee, Juice, and Soda. This allows for more pinpoint accuracy in matching coupons with sale items.

■ **Envelope presorting.** Some couponers find that planning each shopping trip and presorting coupons into envelopes works best for them. The store name and a shopping list are recorded on the outside of the envelope, and the appropriate coupons needed for the trip are placed inside.

You might choose to use a combination of these methods or develop a completely new method of your own. For example, you could plan your shopping trips using the presorting method and carry along a coupon holder in your purse to catch any unadvertised sale opportunities you come across. Ultimately, the more organized you are, the more money you will save.

After you've picked a system of organizing your coupons, the next step is to match your activity to the sales and promotional cycles of the retail stores. One of the best ways to monitor a store's sales is to read through its weekly circulars.

Another is to pick out a few of the items you purchase regularly and track the sales activity each time you are in the store, either mentally noting the rhythms, or taking a second to jot down the price variances from week to week. It only takes a second to record this information, and you will be amazed by the patterns you discover. For example, you may find that your grocery store consistently discounts soup every third week of the month, which means you can plan your purchases accordingly.

Tip: Refer to Chapter 2 for a helpful list of retail clearance cycles. Using your coupons on clearance items can add up to amazing savings.

Rebates

While they may not always offer immediate savings, rebates are a very powerful way to put cash back in your pocket. As we discussed earlier in this chapter, there are two forms of rebates: instant redemption and after-sale redemption.

There are several ways to stay informed about rebates on the products or services you are interested in purchasing. Here are some of the most popular locations to find this information:

- **Product.** The rebate information will be listed directly on, or inside, the packaging.
- **In-store promotion.** The rebate information will be found in the weekly circular, on a rebate slip located on the shelf, or in the store's designated rebate center; it may also print out at the register.
- **Internet.** The rebate information will be supplied on the retailer's website and may be available to print or download after you've purchased the item. You may also find rebate information posted by another Internet user in a forum or on

a "deal board." Here are a few websites to check for current rebates:

- Siteforsavings (www.siteforsavings.com)
- Mwave (www.mwave.com/mwave/rebate.hmx)
- CouponNet (www.couponnet.com)

■ **Manufacturer.** The rebate information will be located on the manufacturer's website, in a periodical advertisement, by calling the manufacturer, or in a direct mailing from the manufacturer.

Just as you keep your coupons organized, it is a good idea to create a system for tracking your rebate activity. A simple notebook or a spreadsheet file on your computer will suffice. A sample of a rebate tracker form for your use can be found at www.momdotcom.net.

In addition, you may want to have a small box, basket, or file folder available in which to store your receipts and paper rebate forms for quick access when you are ready to mail them in. Being organized helps you to make sure you are reimbursed for these rebates.

Mail-In Offers

Often manufacturers will attach an added incentive such as a gift card, toy, coupon, or other product when you purchase their advertised item. Occasionally you will receive this promotional item immediately upon purchase, but more often than not it will be offered in the form of a mail-in promotion. Make sure to send it in before the offer expires. It is also important to note that every once in a while you will come across a mail-in promotion that does not require the purchase of any specific product—these are highly desirable and quite fun to participate in.

You can find out about mail-in promotions the same way you do rebates—on the product, via the Internet, in periodicals, via the manufacturer's website, and on newly released products.

Some mail-in offers require that you pay a modest shipping and handling fee, but more often than not it is well worth the postage to obtain the promotional item. For example, your favorite hot-dog brand offers a promotion wherein you send two UPCs and $1.99 for postage to get a free popular movie on DVD. The $1.99 cost for postage is less than the cost of a typical rental for the movie—well worth the postage to obtain a copy. Even if it is a title that you would not typically be interested in, you may be able to sell it or use it as a gift. Don't ever ignore a mail-in opportunity because it is for an item you personally will not have a use for. You may be overlooking the true value of the item for other money-saving purposes.

Other Forms of Promotions

There are a variety of other promotional offers sponsored by retailers or manufacturers that you should be on the lookout for. Among these are buy-one-get-one-free sales, call-in surveys that offer a code for a reward to be used on a future purchase, and gifts or discounts for enrolling in a credit card program or other services. There are always a variety of creative incentives to heighten customer interest in selected products. The most important thing is just to be aware of the promotions offered and use them to your best possible advantage as a shopper.

Safe Couponing

While searching for coupons online, there are a few things you may wish to avoid. Following is a brief list to help you avoid any pitfalls while perfecting your coupon savvy:

■ **Fraudulent coupons.** Occasionally you will come across a coupon posted on a deal board or a forum that appears to have been scanned by someone; or you may receive a coupon from a friend that looks like it was photocopied or altered in some manner. As you use Internet coupons, you will get a feel for what types of savings are offered by your favorite manufacturers, making it much easier to spot fakes. If it looks suspect, it may well be, and it's best to pass on the offer.

■ **Fees.** Avoid fee-based coupon services. You shouldn't have to pay anyone to receive a coupon. Bottom line: coupons are given out for free by retailers and manufacturers.

■ **Booklets.** Coupon booklet programs allow you to "buy into" the coupon program for a fee, generally around $10 to $25, and in exchange you are given a coupon booklet that allows you to send in a weekly form requesting coupons specific to your shopping needs. This may seem convenient, but there will be additional fees on the back end to take advantage of the program, and ultimately your savings will be minimal. Proceed with caution before getting involved with these types of opportunities and always remember—the whole idea of using coupons is to save money, not to spend money to get the savings.

If you become aware of an online coupon scam, you may contact The Coupon Information Center via mail at The Coupon Information Center, 1020 North Fairfax Street, 6th Floor, Alexandria, VA 22314, or notify the Federal Trade Commission (www.ftc.gov) of your findings.

Follow these steps and look to the resources in the back of this book as your guide for successful couponing. The variety of promotional opportunities available to you as a consumer will bring you and your family a multitude of savings and rewards!

Chapter 5

Store Programs

Store program ('stOr 'prO gram): cool way to get
rewards based on your shopping habits

*I never knew our grocery store offered a baby program
until after we had our last son. One of the clerks handed
me a flyer. What a deal! We've gotten free diapers, discounts on medicine, and even free film development!*

—Margaret, *Ohio*

The Payback of Programs

You have your favorite stores, you go there all the time.
Wouldn't it be great if someone rewarded you for your loyalty?
Many retailers today are doing just that.

To determine which types of programs will work best for
you, let's take a look at the four distinct types of store rewards.

Customer Card Programs

More and more retailers—particularly supermarkets—offer cards that are scanned at the register each time you shop. Using the store's card program typically allows you to take advantage of special pricing and discounts, and you are often able to obtain free items or special coupons toward future purchases.

Generally, there are two ways in which these cards work:

■ **Immediate.** You receive instant rewards or discounts, such as savings on merchandise, free items, or a sweepstakes entry while you are making a purchase.

■ **Cumulative.** Your points are saved over a set amount of time, and when you reach the minimum number of points, you are rewarded with a certificate redeemable for merchandise. For example, if you spend $500 in a five-week period in October and November, you are rewarded with a free turkey just in time for Thanksgiving.

Punch Card Programs

Some retailers offer cards that are punched, stamped, or signed at the register each time you make a purchase. These cards generally have a set value of points you need to accumulate or dollar levels you need to reach, at which time you redeem the card for a valuable discount or free items. Check the cafés and restaurants you go to regularly—you may earn a free coffee or sandwich.

Mail-In Programs

Some retailers offer rebate or mail-in programs to customers. A rebate flyer or list is made available and at the end of each week or month, you simply send in your receipts to get the savings, rebates, or free items offered.

Credit Card Programs

Some retailers offer discounts, delayed billing, interest-free options on big purchases, coupons, or free items for signing up for and using their store-specific credit card. This type of promotion requires you to apply for a card and meet the credit eligibility criteria.

How do you find out about these programs? Many stores have taken the initiative to advertise their reward programs or have a clerk inform you at the time of checkout, but many consumers still remain unaware of the extra advantages available to them for being a frequent shopper at a particular retailer. You may have to do a little investigative work to find out if your store has a program, but don't worry, it will not entail a lot of time or effort on your part to uncover these gems. Try the following proven methods to learn what your stores have to offer in the way of programs:

■ **Ask a store representative.** It may seem a tad simple, but it is often overlooked. The best place to obtain information about store programs is the customer service counter. Ask for information or brochures on any programs available.

■ **Visit the store's website.** Most retailers have a presence on the Web. Look them up by typing the name of each retailer into your favorite search engine and the main website should be among the top sites obtained by your search. Scan the website for information about customer loyalty programs and incentives. You are sure to find a wealth of information and may even be able to enroll online.

■ **Keep an eye out for advertisements.** On your next shopping trip, scan the aisles for brochures, signs, or other identifiers that the store has programs available to their consumers. Fill out any necessary forms and drop them off with the cashier when you check out, or ask the cashier for more information. Also, scan through your local newspaper, particularly the Sunday edition, and you may see announcements or ads regarding special store promotions or programs.

■ **Check out our list of favorites.** To get you started, we've listed a few retailers who offer customer reward programs you might wish to participate in:

- Publix Super Markets (www.publix.com)
- Food Lion (www.foodlion.com)
- CVS/Pharmacy (www.cvs.com)
- Upons (www.upons.com). This online program offers clip-free electronic savings for those who have frequent shopper cards for Kroger, Ralphs, Fry's, King Soopers, Giant Eagle, City Market, Smith's Food & Drug Stores, Dillons, Gerbes, Cala Foods, and Bell Markets.
- Avenue (www.avenue.com)
- Albertsons Family Stores (www.albertsons .com). This grocery/superstore chain includes Jewel/Osco, Sav-On, and Acme Market stores.
- Eckerd (www2.eckerd.com)
- Drugstore.com (www.drugstore.com)
- Amazon Credit Card (www.amazon.com)
- Regal Entertainment Groups (www.regal cinemas.com)

Please note that program guidelines and offerings are subject to change at any time.

A Few Extra Tips

Participating in store programs can mean great savings for you and your family. There are a few things to keep in mind to maximize your savings rather than diminishing them.

■ **Credit card rates.** If you participate in a store's credit card program to take advantage of the free items, discounts, or interest-free periods, find out what the interest rates are (or will be) before fully committing to the program. Some of these cards have exceptionally high interest rates from 19 to 28 percent (possibly higher). If you plan to keep your purchase on the card for an extended period of time, you could wind up paying back your savings in the form of interest charges.

■ **Programs with fees.** Be cautious of store programs that require an upfront fee for you to participate in them. You shouldn't have to pay anything to be considered a loyal and valuable shopper. After all, your continued patronage is very valuable to them to begin with. Take advantage of as many free programs as you can. As long as there are no hidden fees or upfront costs, all you stand to gain is savings.

■ **Requests for social security numbers.** Some store card program applications will request your social security number as a means of identifying you. You are not required by law to release this information. You can write "refused" or "N/A" in the space provided or offer alternatives, such as your driver's license number, instead.

The drawbacks to store programs are minimal and the bulk of programs work to your favor as a consumer. Just be certain to read and understand the terms, sign up for the programs offering you a true benefit, and then sit back and reap the rewards!

Chapter 6

Surveys

Survey ('sir-vA): consumer conglomerates' way of finding out what appeals to you

My husband thought I was nuts when I started surfing the Web looking for paid survey sites. He told me it was all just a bunch of bunk—until the checks started rolling in. Now he wants me to sign him up, too. Men, you gotta love 'em!

—LOIS, *North Dakota*

Surveys Are a Mom's Best Friend

There are a plethora of survey sites on the Internet chomping at the bit to get your opinion on everything from pizza sauce to undergarments. They are so interested in obtaining your opinion that they are willing to pay you for it.

Imagine waking up, puttering around the house in your comfy pajamas, and finding money awaiting you in your e-mail inbox. There will be no boss breathing down your neck or looking over your shoulder. You can keep your fuzzy bunny slippers on and drink your cup of coffee at your leisure. You work on your schedule and participate in only the surveys that you want. Flexibility is, perhaps, the best benefit of this earning opportunity.

Companies will shell out anywhere from $1 to $75 or more, simply for your participation in filling out product surveys. Better yet, you could potentially earn up to $150 dollars for a sixty-minute online focus group or a weeklong participation in a message board study. These corporations need people to give their honest opinions and reactions to marketing concepts. Sound intriguing? We hope so, because there is a bundle of money out there waiting to be made.

You may be asking yourself, what's the catch? Why do they want my opinion? The answer may surprise you, it is so incredibly simple: you are a mom. That's the plain truth of it. Companies want to know what you think because of who you are. Mothers are among the top targeted consumer groups of all time. Women are the primary grocery and retail purchasers in the typical family unit. Why wouldn't major manufacturers want your opinion on new product concepts or existing product lines that they are trying to improve? You do the majority of the buying, so your opinion is of the utmost importance. You are a powerful and savvy shopper.

Companies know that people like us are the lifeblood of their business. Survey agencies want to know what you are thinking, what your likes and dislikes are, and what turns you on and off in the marketplace. Connecting to the source is the best way consumer-oriented companies have to define needs and tailor their products and services to meet shopper demands. Any company incapable of keeping up with consumer expectations would be hard-pressed to stay in business.

In the past, companies used face-to-face focus group studies, telephone surveys, and mail surveys in their attempts to gather feedback and information for business improvement and creative opportunities. Today, with the rise of the Internet, more and more of these companies are turning to the Web for their survey solutions.

Why do these market research firms use Internet surveys? The responses can be tallied within days, sometimes even within hours. Paper-based and telephone surveys require several weeks or months to collect data and tabulate the results. In addition, web surveys reduce the margin for human error and offer a more cost-efficient way to get the same number of responses as from a conventional survey or focus group study. Translation—the company saves bundles of money and is able to pay you more readily for your responses. The company also saves time, which then allows them to bring products and services to the marketplace faster, thereby enriching your life with the benefits of new developments. And you get the satisfaction of knowing your input helped facilitate the process.

I was at the market the other day and noticed Healthy Choice had several new frozen dinners. Imagine my surprise when I realized that three of them were ones I voted for in a survey I did three months ago. How cool is that?

—SANDY, *Arizona*

Now that you understand the basics of why survey companies are interested in you, are you ready to make some money? Then read on!

Before you sign up with survey websites, you should consider the different forms of compensation and the different types of surveys offered by research companies. Some surveys have brief questionnaires that can be completed in a short amount of time. Others will have more involved questions and entail a significant time commitment. Multiple compensation avenues exist as well. There are surveys that pay out by cash or check, surveys that tender payment in the form of gift certificates, and even some that may not seem to "pay" you at all.

It is important to prioritize your focus before enrolling with oodles of survey companies. If it's not a good match to start, then neither you nor the company will truly benefit from the relationship.

Let's take an in-depth look at the different types of survey methods and payment options available to you.

Prescreeners and Qualifiers

Many research companies will send you a presurvey, referred to as a prescreener or qualifier. These minisurveys are quick and easy to complete. Generally, they will ask a few demographic questions and a few lifestyle questions. Some will offer a few points toward earning prizes, cash, or an entry into a monthly raffle, others will offer no up-front compensation. Screeners are designed to ensure you fit a certain profile or demographic before you complete the full version of the survey. All surveyors have a specific group of people in mind for each and every survey conducted. For example, if the company requests a survey study on diapers and you have no small children, you may not qualify. Another survey candidate, a mother with a six-month-old child in the home, would be the ideal choice.

Qualifiers prevent you from wasting your time on surveys you would have no interest in, as well as serving as an easy elimination tool for the research company. Always take the time to complete the qualifiers you receive. Each of them may earn you the chance to participate in a more lucrative opportunity. Another way of looking at it: while you may only get an entry into the monthly survey website raffle for completing the prescreener, you might get the chance to participate in a $20 cash-paying survey based on your responses.

Sweepstake Entry Surveys

Sweepstake entry surveys offer compensation in the form of an entry in a drawing in which you can win one of a set number of monetary prizes. While you may not realize an instant payback, these surveys are not without merit. They are usually quick and entertaining, and you never know—you could be a lucky winner. The more sweepstake surveys you complete, the better your odds of being rewarded with a cash incentive. A potential reward of $100 for completing thirty minutes worth of short surveys in a month is an excellent gamble to take. Your odds of winning are fair, as each survey has a limit on participants. After the required quota of surveys is completed, the company will close the survey to further submissions.

Cash Surveys

The surveys we are all looking for are the ones that pay cash. They have a set value and will state the dollar award clearly at the start of the survey. Usually these surveys can be completed in less than twenty minutes, and payment arrives via snail mail. Occasionally a survey will run longer, and in most cases compensation is adjusted accordingly. Most are on a pay-per-survey basis. There are a few companies that bank your earnings until you reach a certain level (usually between $10 and $15) before you are able to request payment. This simply keeps the company from having to spend an excessive amount to issue small-sum checks.

A small number of survey companies also offer cash compensation to your Paypal online account. Paypal (www

.paypal.com) is a payment option company offering accounts for your use on the Internet.

Gift Certificate Surveys

You will find that some surveys pay in electronic gift certificates; among the most popular are those from Amazon.com. These gift certificates arrive in your e-mail inbox. The time frame for payment is usually specified prior to the start of the survey. Though you may be slightly tempted to scoff at these opportunities, the reality is that they may save you big money in the long run. Consider that a company like Amazon.com sells a huge variety of popular entertainment and household products. The accumulative value of your gift certificates could cover a chunk of your Christmas shopping for the year or purchase that new DVD player your family has been hoping for.

Point Surveys

Point surveys are surveys that reward you with a set number of points for your time. The points are then banked, and you are later able to redeem them for cash or merchandise in accordance with the reward level you have achieved for the particular retailers' point program. As a general rule of thumb, 1,000 points is typically equivalent to $10. The point scale is equal to the time invested in the survey—the longer the survey, the more points earned. When you have reached the allotted point level and are ready to redeem, it simply takes a few clicks of your mouse at the retailers' website, and your reward will be on its way to your door.

In addition to cash and merchandise rewards, some of the point survey websites also offer you the opportunity to use your points for raffles, donations to charities, or occasional special offers like hotel accommodations.

Product Evaluation Surveys

Would you like to participate in an evaluation of a new cereal? A child's toy? Perhaps even perfumes or body lotions? Product testing is another way to benefit from Internet surveys. With a product evaluation survey, you receive a product in the mail to evaluate for a set period of time. After the trial period has ended, you will be asked to follow up with an online survey or a phone interview to give your feedback on the product. Expressing your opinions to help shape the future of the product is exciting for you and highly beneficial to the manufacturer. How fascinating to walk into your local retailer to find the results of your product study on the shelf! Many of these evaluation surveys also offer monetary compensation on completion, providing you with the best of both worlds. If nothing else, you get to try a new and innovative product free of charge, which carries with it a savings to you. For example, suppose you are asked to try a new laundry detergent and offer your feedback on the product. Participating in this offer will put the $8 to $10 you would have spent on laundry detergent at the supermarket back into your pocket, thereby allowing you extra funds for other purchases.

Live Chat Groups

Chat group surveys offer research companies a more in-depth way to evaluate concepts and products. They are extra-intensive in comparison to a regular electronic survey and generally require a half hour to an hour or more of your time. However, you will be well compensated for any time spent in a focus group. Generally a $35 to $50 incentive is the average payout for thirty minutes. Upward of $75 to $100 is a common payout for longer, hour-length chat group studies. These surveys are conducted in live chat rooms with you, a moderator, and other participants. You may be asked to express your thoughts and opinions on the subject of the project, or you may find yourself brainstorming ideas for a general topic. In principle, chat group surveys are engaging, rewarding, and lucrative experiences.

Focus Group Surveys

Guided by a moderator, forum focus groups are similar to live chat surveys. The big difference is that focus groups are conducted on a fixed forum board rather than in a live chat room. The fixed forum board atmosphere allows for participants to access the survey when it is convenient for them and offers the ability to review and keep up with ideas posted by other participants in the survey.

Focus groups also pay better than your average survey, and they require you to log on to a message board and respond to questions set up by a moderator for a specified number of days. The pay for these studies is usually in the $50 to $100 range, but depending on the length of the project, they can potentially pay even more. The most important thing to remember about these groups is to be thorough. Be certain to answer all the questions with detailed and complete thoughts, otherwise you may find the company responsible for the group is unwilling to compensate you. The survey firm is paying big bucks with the expectation that you will complete the project with enthusiasm and due diligence.

There are no limits to the number or types of surveys you can participate in. Typically, the number of survey opportunities will correspond with the number of survey companies with which you choose to register. It will also depend on the amount of information you provide to them and your demographic profile. The more information you provide about yourself and your family, the more opportunities you will receive in the long run. You can't lose.

How Do I Find the Companies That Pay?

How do you determine which survey sites are worth your time and which are not? To start with, you can rest assured that the sites listed in this book are tried and true and have paid as promised in all of our dealings with them. We are panelists with many of these companies and to this day receive compensation for our participation.

When you start surfing the Net and finding companies on your own, it may be trial and error. Like any other job search, you are going to have to invest a little bit of time and energy applying to companies. Once you are an applicant in their database, the research firms will send you e-mails inviting you to take paid surveys.

When you take a survey and receive your payout as promised, you know you have a winner. If you fill out a survey application and get nothing but spam, do not waste your time on anything this company has to offer. If they don't pay, you won't play. Again, with the flexibility of this moneymaking venture, you are in complete control of what and how much you choose to do.

Follow this three-step process to get moving on your new-found career as a survey panelist.

1. Begin with the Big Guys

We would be remiss if we did not provide you with a best-of-the-best list. For the record, we suggest that you begin by familiarizing yourself with these survey companies and start participating in a number of their surveys before moving on to signing up with other researchers. This way, you will have a basic understanding of what to expect and will more readily be able to spot a subpar survey company or a scam, should you encounter one.

The following are well-established survey companies on the Internet (listed in no particular order) that have proven to deliver as promised. We have also listed a few tips and details about each surveyor to serve as a guide, though as with every business, the details are subject to change.

- National Family Opinion (NFO) (www.mysurvey.com). NFO offers a variety of survey opportunities that pay out in points. The points are accumulated and can be turned in for cash, products, and a variety of other choices.
- American Consumer Opinion (www.acop.com). American Consumer Opinion is owned and operated by Decision Analyst, Inc., a major international marketing research firm. They offer a variety of survey and online focus group opportunities that pay out in free products, cash, checks, and gifts. There are also opportunities to participate in monthly drawings and special drawings for cash prizes.
- Greenfield Online (www.signup.greenfieldonline.com). Greenfield Online offers a wealth of survey opportunities via e-mail and on their website. A good habit with Greenfield is to check their website daily to find new survey opportunities. They offer cash incentives and opportunities to participate in monthly sweepstakes for cash prizes.
- Gozing Survey (www.gozingsurvey.com). Gozing Survey pays cash for participation through Paypal, gift certificates to Buy.com, or sweepstakes opportunities for completing online movie and product surveys.
- Survey Savvy (www.surveysavvy.com). Survey Savvy is the online division of Luth Research, a leader in market research for twenty-five years. They offer cash incentives for surveys and sweepstakes drawing opportunities.
- Synovate (www.synovate.com). To sign up for Synovate, go to the main website and check under the Contacts link. You will find current information and an e-mail address to initiate registration. The company offers a variety of survey opportu-

nities that pay with cash incentives, free products, and entries in monthly drawings for cash prizes.

- Keynote (www.keynote.com). Keynote is a new breed of survey company. They help businesses measure and improve the customer experience on their websites. Keynote offers the opportunity to participate in online interactive studies. For each evaluation completed, they typically pay in the form of Amazon.com gift certificates.

2. Access Your Resources

After visiting, registering, and testing some of the well-known survey companies, the next best measure is to seek out information from those you know. Ask your friends if they have experience with any research companies, find out who they are, and sign up. Ask other moms on the Internet what survey companies they have heard of or have had success with. Check out Chapter 10 for detailed information on how to access peer resources via the Internet.

3. Tackle the Internet

Maxed out your resources? Then search for some of the lesser known survey companies on your own and see what they have to offer. Branch out and find additional survey companies to sign up with. The bottom line: the Internet is an ever-changing and growing entity, and new opportunities to make money surface almost daily. We could not possibly provide you with a complete and comprehensive list, because as you read this, new companies are emerging and looking for potential survey takers.

Once again, that handy search engine comes into play. Typing something as simple as "paid surveys" or "list of survey sites" into a search engine will leave you with almost ninety pages of search results. From there you can weed through and find emerging and existing opportunities to gain even more income.

It may go without saying, but we will stress it again: do not fall prey to any website that charges you to participate in online survey opportunities. The object is to get paid for your opinion, not to pay someone else to provide information for you.

Now That I Have Found the Survey Companies, What's Next?

On each survey website you encounter, be sure to read the individual site's policies and Frequently Asked Questions (FAQ) section. You want to be certain the site is set up in a professional manner and answers most of the basic questions you have about the company. The basic questions you want addressed should include, but not be limited to, the following:

- **Do I have to participate in every survey?** This is a good question to ask up front as some companies may require your constant participation in their program or you may find yourself dropped from their database. In all fairness, most of the survey companies will want to see your active participation in completing projects. It is how they get results and how you reap the rewards. However, you want to be sure you are dealing with a company that understands occasionally you may be unable to take part in a given survey.
- **If I cannot finish a survey, what do I do?** Find out if there are penalties for not completing the survey. Will you lose the opportunity to get paid for the survey if you get interrupted and are not able to complete it? Will you be able to pause the survey and go back to it at a later time? While this is not of the utmost importance and will be a unique situation if it arises, it is nice to know the company you are working

with has a friendly attitude toward the realities of life that occur from time to time.

■ **How many memberships per household can I have?** If only one person per household is allowed to join, by all means sign yourself up and do not walk away from the opportunity. The reason you will want to investigate this area is so you do not miss the opportunity to register additional family members, thereby allowing them to earn income opportunities along with you.

■ **Is my personal information safe?** This is a question that you do not want to take lightly. A reputable survey company will list the measures it takes to secure your private information. They will list clearly whether they share your personal statistics, address, or other pertinent information with other entities. Once you know the facts, you can decide whether you are comfortable with their policies or not. If they do not offer any facts regarding privacy, you may want to contact their customer support group to obtain the information or pass on the offer.

■ **What is the survey company's spam policy?** Check out the company's policies regarding spam and find out whether they participate in selling your e-mail address or information to other companies. Refer to Chapter 12 for complete details about what spam is and how it can affect you.

■ **How do I get paid?** This is the biggie! Always find out up front what and how the company will pay you. In addition, find out how you will be able to access your money or rewards. You wouldn't accept a job without knowing when your paycheck was coming or how much you were going to be paid per hour. The same should hold true when you are signing up with a research company. Remember that you are a self-employed agent and need to be able to budget accordingly.

■ **When do I get paid?** Will they pay you within twenty-four hours or twenty-four days? This is an important factor when determining whether to participate with a particular survey company. If the company pays out every six months for participation, it could be a long wait to reap the rewards of your efforts. The reliable companies will usually reward you within a two- to six-week period. They know your time and input is valuable, and they want to ensure your continued participation.

■ **What happens if I do not receive my payment or prize?** Does the company have a program in place to address concerns or nonpayment issues? Is there an easily identifiable customer service support option available? It is prudent to find out in the beginning if support will be available should the need arise.

■ **Do they have a referral program?** Many survey companies do not offer incentives for referrals. While it is not a necessity for the company to offer one, it is a good practice to find out if they have such a program. That way when you share the wealth with family and friends, you will be able to reap the rewards of your good deeds.

■ **Do they have a customer service number I call?** As addressed in some of the earlier questions, finding out if there are adequate customer service options available to support you will be an invaluable asset. Should you ever be in need of assistance, it will be comforting to know there is a team available to help you. Clear customer service options also distinguish the fly-by-night companies from the dependable researchers you will want to work with.

If you are unable to find the answers you are looking for in the FAQ section of the website, do not hesitate to contact the company via e-mail or telephone. The timely nature of their response and the way they handle your question should tell you a lot about how legitimate and friendly the company is. You would not want to deal with an establishment that gives you the runaround on the telephone or answers you with a form letter rather then addressing your concerns. Reputable companies want to help you to the best of their ability, because they want you and your valuable opinions on their panels.

Among the legitimate survey companies, there are a few less than desirable companies you should be leery of. The undesirables would like you to pay a "one-time fee" for access to their survey database. For your money, they offer to set you up in their database and promise that in no time you will be rolling in dough. As a general rule, you will not have to shell out money to make money doing surveys on the Internet. Not all of these services are completely bogus, but there are plenty of reputable companies that do not require you to pay to participate in surveys. It is a wise practice to avoid the companies that do charge.

Along the same lines, there are websites out there that charge you for lists of companies that do paid surveys online. Let us assure you that these are to be avoided at all cost. It is absurd to pay for information that is readily available for free, once you know how to find it.

Additional Tips and Information

Once you have located a company you think will be a good fit for you, and you understand what types of surveys and payment options they provide, signing up is generally a pain-free process. In most cases it will be as simple as filling out your name and address, a brief interests section, and a demographic profile. All of this information is needed by the surveyor so they know what types of surveys to send you. This process is comparable to finding your perfect mate through a dating service; in theory, the more you have in common, the more compatible you are apt to be.

For example, if you are an eighteen-year-old female, it is unlikely that you will be asked to complete a survey on menopause products. This saves the survey companies time, and saves you time and headaches by keeping your inbox from filling up with incompatible survey opportunities.

Here are a few other tips to keep in mind when signing up with new survey websites.

Set Up a Survey Account

We strongly urge you to register a separate e-mail account to use solely for surveys. You don't want to be digging through an inbox full of spam, personal e-mails, or other offers searching for your paid survey prospects. You could conceivably miss out on opportunities to make money because you overlooked the invitation e-mail. An e-mail account specifically set up for surveys can ensure that you will not overlook or accidentally delete an important message, and everything will be in one place so you know where to find all your survey–related correspondence.

Get Your Family Involved

If a company's terms of service allow it, you will want to consider registering everyone in your immediate family capable of participating in survey opportunities. These companies want to reach a variety of people. They need your husband's opinion on razor blades and lawn mowers. They may want your teenage daughter's opinion on her favorite shampoo.

Start new the key point to stress here is to only sign up individuals within your family unit who can realistically complete a survey. Unfortunately, this means you should avoid assigning your thirteen-month-old daughter or her pet hamster an account. It is important, however, to include your infants, toddlers, and pets under your own profile. The survey companies occasionally want to know whether Fido likes the dog biscuit samples they sent you or what brand of diapers suits your baby the best.

I can hardly believe someone paid me fifteen bucks to tell them what cat litter Pouncer prefers. I guess he's earning his keep after all!

—Marian, *Missouri*

Stay Tuned to Opportunities

Check your survey e-mail daily. Check the survey websites that have regular online openings daily as well. We cannot stress enough the importance of checking your survey e-mail account as often as you can. Many surveys are quota based, and most of the time these quotas are filled quickly. One of the worst feelings is to see that money sitting in your inbox, then clicking the link only to find out the quota has been filled. It happens to the best of us, but with vigilance, checking that e-mail will help prevent it from happening to you.

Record Your Income

As the surveys start rolling in, it is prudent to keep a journal or notepad near the computer in which to log your efforts for the day. That way you are able to keep track of the checks you are expecting, as well as a rough figure of your earnings for the month. Also keep in mind that these companies will not be providing you with a W-2 form at tax time. As a survey participant, it is your responsibility to track your earnings. You are a self-employed agent. If you find you are earning enough money to catch the attention of Uncle Sam, it is your duty to inform the Internal Revenue Service (IRS) of your earnings. Be certain to consult the IRS website (www.irs.gov) for complete guidelines and regulations for reporting self-employed income. To your benefit, as a self-employed individual, you may also find that there will be acceptable tax deductions, such as claiming an approved portion of your monthly Internet access bill or the supplies used to record your earnings. Make sure you read through the IRS information and thoroughly understand all the implications and benefits of being self-employed. Another excellent resource is your regular tax accountant or attorney for advice and an understanding of the laws.

Keep an Eye Out for the Elusive

There are several survey sites out there that cannot be accessed via a search engine or a referral, so becoming a panelist with them is much more difficult then at a typical site. There is only one way to become a member of these "special" companies; they will solicit you. How do you get them to solicit you? As you begin to take surveys, you are often asked to elaborate on some of your simple answers. For example, if you state you definitely would not buy the product being discussed in the survey, they may ask in the next question why you would not buy it, followed by the key words "be specific." When you are posed this question, answer to the best of your ability and be creative. When you consistently put forth the extra effort, your account may be flagged and presented to one of these invitation-only companies. They are looking for dynamic panelists, and with smaller databases, they are able to offer higher compensation more consistently. Bottom line: be specific, be complete, and be creative; it will be worth it.

Don't Shy Away from Opportunities

Are you concerned that because you live outside of the United States that you won't be eligible for many surveys? Don't be pessimistic. The Internet has brought on a global revolution for many organizations. Companies are now seeking a lot of information and desperately need data to understand their new markets of opportunity. You may have more opportunities available than you dreamed possible. There is only one way to find out—register with the survey companies and give it a try.

In reality, you have nothing to lose, only a potentially rewarding career to gain.

Beware of Spin-Off Scams

A popular tagalong to survey opportunities come from companies that falsely broadcast themselves as marketing research
companies. These false-impression companies will snag you
into participating by offering to pay you for reading your
e-mail or for allowing them access to study your online surfing habits. When you sign up with these so-called survey companies and give them your e-mail address, demographic
information, and lifestyle profile, you are really helping their
business build a rich database of information. In turn, the
company will use all the information in the database to attract
advertisers who want to focus their advertising to a specified
group of individuals; for example, mothers with children
under the age of five. Those advertisers pay the company who
harvested your information to send an e-mail to the targeted
group. What happens then? You get a spam buildup in your
inbox and will never see a legitimate survey or moneymaking
opportunity.

You may be offered three to five cents per e-mail to read
and click on an advertiser's link in order for the company to
validate that you actually read through the e-mail. The catch
is that you are not eligible to receive payment until you accumulate a set dollar amount that is typically in the $50 to $100
range. That payout may seem attractive at the onset, but if you
do the math, you will have to spend around sixty-two hours
to read approximately 2,500 e-mails before you can reach a
$50 payout level. If being paid an average of eighty cents per
hour for your time sounds attractive, then you may benefit
from these types of companies. We would further caution you
to verify that you will, indeed, get paid for your time by using
the same guidelines for researching companies found earlier
in this chapter.

Get Paid for Referrals

Now that you are making money doing paid surveys, your friends and family will probably want to know what your secret is. You can reap further benefits by introducing them to the paid survey world via referrals. Referrals allow those you invite to partake in this moneymaking venture, while providing you with additional income at the same time. Some companies that have a referral program pay you for activity in your referrals account. In other words, if the people you refer complete a survey, you get paid. These companies may also offer a set payment for referrals, or if it is a point system, a set number of points. No matter how the payment is received, you benefit from referrals.

Companies that offer a referral program generally have the information readily available in an easy-to-understand format. When you click on the Referrals link, you will usually be taken to a page that either allows you to enter your friends' and family's e-mail addresses, or you will be provided with a referral link that you can send out from your own e-mail account. Just remember, never send these links or e-mails to anyone unless you are confident they are interested in receiving them, otherwise your e-mail will fall into the category of spam, which, as you will find out, is illegal and incredibly annoying to those who receive it.

Following the tips and guidelines presented in this chapter will have you well on your way to a lucrative income in no time. Educated choices and solid research will afford you greater opportunities in the future. Remember, above all else, have fun with each and every survey you encounter. You have so much to gain from participating in market research, and the research companies have so much to gain from you. It's definitely a winning situation for all!

Chapter 7
Mystery Shopping

Mystery shopper ('mis-tah rE 'shä- pur): a highly aware
consumer who defies explanation

*I can take the kids along, meet my best friend at the mall
for lunch, and get paid for the trip. What could be
better?*

—BECKY, *North Dakota*

Who Said There's No Such Thing as a Free Lunch?

Wouldn't you love to walk into your favorite department store
and tell them how to run their business? Better yet, wouldn't
it be great if they really listened? To top it all off, what if they
paid you for your time and feedback? Companies all around
the globe are willing to do just that. The job title is commonly

referred to as "mystery shopper" or "mystery guest," and it can be an extremely rewarding career.

Companies will typically pay from $5 to $100 or more per assignment to have you "shop" their location and tell them what they are doing right as well as what they are doing wrong when it comes to their products and customer service. These companies need impartial people to critique their business so they can have a better understanding of what works and what they need to improve. And the best part is that the jobs keep coming as the products, services, and management structures change. Constant information is necessary to help companies grow and evolve.

The basic job description: a person who poses as an "ordinary" consumer for the purpose of evaluating a business and afterward provides a written or verbal report. Does this sound like something you are interested in? Take this simple test to find out if you have the basic instincts to be a successful mystery shopper:

1.	Do you like to shop?	YES	NO
2.	Do you like to eat out?	YES	NO
3.	Do you interact well with others?	YES	NO
4.	Can you keep a secret?	YES	NO
5.	Are you able to recognize high-quality service?	YES	NO
6.	Do you have a good memory?	YES	NO
7.	Do you have adequate writing skills?	YES	NO
8.	Would you like to make money while you run your daily errands?	YES	NO

Scoring: Give yourself 1 point for each Yes response.

Mystery Maybe (1–3 Yes responses): Mystery shopping may not be a main focus for you, but don't despair. These assignments require different skill sets and knowledge, and there is still money to be earned. Read on.

Mystery Ma'am (4–6 Yes responses): You are off to a great start and will continue to build on the basics as you complete assignments. Keep reading to discover what awaits you.

Mystery Diva (7 or more Yes responses): You were born to be a mystery shopper! Read ahead to gather all the information you need to continue on your path.

Where Do I Begin?

Before you sign up to be a mystery shopper, you should consider the different forms of compensation and the different types of shopping assignments you will encounter. Some opportunities have detailed requirements and involve significant time commitments; some only require a small purchase, brief questionnaire, or short amount of time. Different compensation structures exist as well. Some companies pay up front, and others pay through reimbursement.

It is important to understand the differences and to prioritize your focus before enrolling with oodles of mystery shopper organizations. Just as with surveys, if it is not a good match to start, neither you nor the company will truly benefit from the relationship.

There are four main categories of mystery shopping assignments:

■ **Store.** These jobs range from shopping a supermarket for a particular brand of ketchup to purchasing and returning an item at a children's clothing store. Some companies will have you assess a particular area of the store, and others will ask for a comprehensive report on the entire building, including the parking area.

■ **Restaurant.** These jobs range from purchasing a beverage through the drive-through of a fast-food location to ordering a three-course meal for two at an upscale restaurant. Some companies will have you primarily assess the service, and others will ask for a detailed analysis of the food, environment, servers, and facility—often including the restrooms.

■ **Online.** This is a diverse area of mystery guest shopping, and it is still expanding. Assignments may include e-mailing customer service with an issue or purchasing and returning an item through the mail. Some companies will ask you to give your overall impression of the website, and others will ask for particulars right down to the postmark information on your package and even may request electronic photographs of the package.

■ **Phone.** These jobs typically involve testing some service area of a company, but they may include a catalog purchase of an item. Some companies will provide you with a detailed script to use, and others will prefer that you record your conversations in writing, noting times and key events.

The types of shopping assignments you participate in will depend on your preferences, resources, and the companies you choose to enroll with. There are no limits to how many assignments you can complete, other than the reality of what your time and resources will allow. However, the companies you work for may impose limits such as the number of times you can mystery shop a single location. For example, if you mystery shop a particular store for sales and returns too often, the store employees will begin to recognize you and may question why you are returning items on a regular basis. If your cover as a mystery shopper is blown, the impact of your visit diminishes dramatically. Therefore companies may impose set limits on the number of times you can complete a similar assignment in the same location.

Once you have determined what types of mystery shopping assignments you are interested in, it is important to understand the different types of compensation and decide which ones you are comfortable with. There are four main ways a company will choose to compensate mystery shopper employees.

■ **Cash allowance.** Companies may offer a set amount of money for your time, effort, and possibly product purchase prior to your completion of the assignment. While this situation is ideal, it is uncommon. Why? Like any other job, your employer does not usually give you a paycheck before you complete the work week(s). Mystery shopping is a job, and you will be an employee of the company that requests your participation in the assignment. Occasionally, however, a check will be issued prior to a mystery shop that includes the dollars you will need to complete the assignment and often a set amount extra to pay for your time and feedback.

■ **Reimbursement.** The bulk of mystery shopping assignments work with a reimbursement program. You are usually given set instructions, including a detailed breakdown of cost allowance, such as how much you can spend for your food entrée and how much pay you will receive for completing a questionnaire about your shopping experience. During your assignment, you need to keep all receipts and are responsible for paying expenses with your charge card or cash on hand. After the assignment, you submit your receipts along with any other required materials to the company, and they reimburse you for the expenses along with a predetermined payment for your time, generally by issuing you a check on their payment schedule.

■ **Payroll.** Some companies keep their mystery shoppers on their general payroll, and you receive a weekly, biweekly, or monthly check as long as you are completing your assignments as agreed. The majority of companies that use this form of payment are those requesting you to complete phone assignments.

■ **Voucher.** In some instances, a company may issue you a gift certificate or other form of voucher to pay for the services or product at the facility you are mystery shopping. Generally the certificate will be issued in a standard amount so as not to arouse the suspicion of the employee accepting the voucher. If there is a remaining balance on the voucher, you may be required to send it back to the company along with your assessment or other required materials.

Though there are four main forms of compensation, you may find that you are offered a combination or even an alternate form, such as being able to keep the product you purchase. In addition to these forms of compensation, there are often other perks attached. Restaurants, in particular, generally reimburse you for food and for filling out a feedback form describing your experience. You are paid for the assignment, plus you get to enjoy a free meal.

Now that you understand the types of assignments available and the forms of compensation, it is time to find the good-quality companies.

Where Do I Sign?

I've been renting videos from the same video store for years now. Who knew that I could have been watching my movies for free? Now that I'm a mystery shopper, I get to rent two DVDs a week and as long as I report my feedback on time, I get the money I paid for the rentals reimbursed, plus I get paid enough extra to splurge on popcorn and treats for the kids. Amazing!

—DONNA, *Delaware*

Where do you find mystery shopping companies, and how do you figure out which of them are worth applying to? The Internet is a prime place to begin your search, and once you are settled in and working for some of the larger firms, you may want to begin making inquiries with local companies as well. One step at a time though. Let's take a look at how to find mystery shopping opportunities through the Internet and how to determine whether you want to fill out an application with a specific company.

When you start surfing the Net and finding companies on your own, it may be trial and error. Like any other job search, you will have to invest a little bit of time and energy applying to companies. You may be required to complete a few simple tests; keep in mind that you are applying for a job. Mystery shopping can be a very lucrative career, and companies want to know that they are signing on a serious-minded employee who is going to put forth their best effort to get the job done.

If you are turned down by a particular company for some reason, do not stop your search. Just as when you're seeking work at a local business, it is all about matching the employee to the company that fits. You may find that you are not a good match for one company and a great match for two others.

Follow this four-step process to begin your mystery shopping career.

1. Begin with the Big Guys

As we did in Chapter 6, we would like to give you a solid starting point for mystery shopper agencies with whom you may want to consider forming a relationship. To the best of our knowledge, these companies have good practices, although we cannot guarantee this as their terms are subject to change. We suggest that you begin by familiarizing yourself with these mystery shopping companies and participating in a number of their assignments before moving on to signing up with other companies. You will then have a basic understanding of what to expect and will more readily be able to spot a subpar company or a scam, should you encounter one.

The following are well-established mystery shopping companies that have a presence on the Internet:

- Mystery Guest, Inc. (www.mysteryguestinc.com)
- A Closer Look (www.a-closer-look.com)
- Service Intelligence Secret ShopNet (www.secretshop net.com)
- Corporate Research International Mystery Shops (www .mysteryshops.com)

2. Access Your Resources

After working for some of the well-known mystery shopping companies, the next step is to seek information from those you know. Ask your friends if they have experience with any mystery shopping companies, find out what they are, and apply. Ask other moms on the Internet what mystery shopping companies they have heard of or had success with. Take a look at Chapter 10 for detailed information on how to access peer resources via the Internet.

3. Tackle the Internet

Have you maxed out your resources? Then search for some of the lesser known mystery shopping companies and see what they have to offer. The bottom line is the Internet and the business worlds are always changing and growing. New companies and opportunities crop up regularly. We could not possibly provide you with a complete and comprehensive list, because as you read this, a new company is emerging and looking for potential mystery shoppers.

Do not sign up with any website that charges you to obtain mystery guest company information. The object is to get paid, not to pay someone else to provide your information for you. Quality organizations will advertise and place their information with the major search engines such as Google. You should not have to pay someone else to find out where to apply.

4. Shop Your Own Backyard

Once you have completed an assignment or two and have experience as a mystery shopper, polish your résumé and start phoning or mailing your local company headquarters to find out if they are in need of mystery shoppers. For example, perhaps you have a national retailer such as Target or Circuit City nearby. Do a quick search on the Internet to find their corporate information and contact their human resource department to inquire about a mystery shopping position. A typical phone inquiry might go something like this:

> *You:* "Hello. My name is Sue Smith, and I'm calling to inquire whether you are currently hiring for mystery shopper positions. Is there a representative available that I might speak with?"

> *XYZ Company Operator:* "Sure, I'll connect you to our human resource department. One moment, please."

> *XYZ Company HR Representative:* "Hello, this is Darren, XYZ human resource supervisor. How may I help you?"

> *You:* "Hello, Darren. My name is Sue Smith, and I'm calling to find out whether you use mystery shopping agents, and if you might be accepting applications for such positions."

XYZ Company HR Representative: "Well, Ms. Smith, we do have a mystery shopping program, but we do not hire the agents through this office, we outsource the work."

You: "May I ask which company you use, and if you have any contact information so that I might apply with them directly?"

XYZ Company HR Representative: "Sure, I'll look that information up for you right now."

Although this is a mock representation, you will be able to use a similar approach with any company you deem a prospect for possible mystery shopping assignments. As in this example, you will find that many companies use firms that specialize in mystery shopping; you may even be employed by the company they use. If this is the case, be sure to let your mystery shopping employer know that you are interested in future assignments with the XYZ Company. If you are not employed by the mystery shopping company they use, you have just found a great new opportunity to explore.

What's the Next Step?

The first step you will take is to fill out the application and perhaps answer a survey about a recent shopping experience you've had. You may be asked to take a short test to assess how well you follow instructions and remember details. There are several "desirable" skills that mystery shopping companies look for. Among the primary qualifications are prior customer service or retail experience, a demonstrated ability to follow instructions, and good verbal and written communication skills. For field mystery shopping assignments, you will need to provide your own transportation, so a vehicle is necessary to make the most of your opportunities.

Each company you encounter will be looking for different types of shoppers. Some may be seeking mystery shoppers who have children or pets, and some may be seeking shoppers who are available to travel to shop hotels and airlines. Be sure to find out as much information as you can about the company by reading through their website or contacting their main office prior to filling out an application. Obtaining this information before applying will also allow you to put your best foot forward and tailor your information to best illustrate that you have the skill set and availability they are looking for.

Also be sure to read through or call to find out the individual company's policies. Read through the Frequently Asked Questions (FAQ) section on the website or telephone the employee/customer service department to ask. You want to be certain the company and website is set up in a professional manner and that most of the basic questions you have are answered. The questions you want addressed should include, but not be limited to, the following:

- What types of mystery guest assignments does the company offer?
- What type of compensation does the company offer?
- If I cannot finish an assignment, what happens?
- How many assignments can I participate in per week/month/year?
- Will my personal information be shared with other companies?
- How frequently will I be paid?
- What happens if I do not receive my compensation as expected?
- Is there an employee contact to answer my questions?

If you don't find the answers you are looking for in the FAQ section of the website, do not hesitate to contact the company via e-mail or telephone. Reputable companies want to help you to the best of their ability, because they want you to succeed as a mystery shopper.

I Have My First Assignment, Now What?

Congratulations, you've been hired by XYZ Company to be a mystery shopping agent. But what comes next? While each mystery shopping company operates a little differently, for the most part, you will need to follow some or all of the following steps.

Obtain Your Assignment

Some companies will provide you with a detailed shopping schedule, especially if you are working for a single company. For example, you may be expected to visit a fast-food restaurant once a week and evaluate the facility and service. Other companies may call you with assignments that match your profile or require you to search their database frequently to apply for assignments that match your interests. If you are employed by a company that requires an application for each assignment, it is important to keep an eye out for assignments in your area and respond promptly. Assignments are given on a first-come, first-served basis. A little diligence on your part will pay off.

Understand Your Assignment

With each shopping assignment you should receive clear instructions about what is expected of you on the location visit. These guidelines and expectations are very important.

You will receive information such as when to arrive, what areas you need to assess, what you need to purchase, and other important duties expected of you as a mystery shopper, including what to wear and what to say. If you do not receive a clear set of instructions, it is in your best interest to contact your employer and discuss the details of the assignment. Following the proper guidelines will ensure that you are paid for the assignment. If you do not perform the job in accordance with the company's expectations, you could run the risk of not receiving compensation for your work.

Complete Your Assignment

Be sure to follow the guidelines and record your observations accurately and thoroughly. The more comprehensive your feedback, the more it will help the company you are assessing. As a result, you will gain favor with your employer, which may lead to more and often bigger assignments. Mystery shopping employers operate the same as any regular company does; they prefer to promote and give assignments to representatives they trust will do the best job.

Get Paid for Your Assignment

An excellent practice is to keep a mystery shopping assignment journal. In the journal, record the date of your assignment, the type of assignment, receipt information, expected reimbursement (or in some cases, the amount of reimbursement you have already received), and the date your compensation is received. This journal will be an invaluable tool for tracking payments and ensuring that you receive accurate reimbursement. It will also allow you to follow up with the company easily should you find you are missing a payment. Just as you would check a standard paycheck each week to make sure you received the right amount for the correct number of hours worked, you should get in the habit of verifying your mystery shopping compensation.

The journal will also be handy at tax time. As a mystery shopper, you will be responsible for reporting your income in accordance with your state and federal tax laws. Many mystery shopping companies may not provide you with end-of-year tax forms, so you will find that keeping accurate records of your income and expenses will be very useful to you.

Additional Tips for Mystery Shopping Success

Here are a few more "insider" tips to further help you with your mystery shopping endeavors:

- **Start slow.** Get a feel for the jobs you like performing and expand from there. You do not want to overload yourself until you have a full understanding of the industry.
- **Run periodic searches.** Locate additional mystery shopping organizations by typing "mystery shopping" into your favorite search engine. Check regularly as new opportunities arise all the time.
- **Check in with other shoppers.** Find Internet message boards pertaining to mystery shopping for proven tips and tricks. This will also connect you with other mystery shoppers to share experiences and likes/dislikes about the industry. See Chapter 10 for more information on finding forums.
- **Stay organized.** Having a system will make your mystery shopping experiences easier and more pleasurable. Make note of all the important details surrounding your mystery shopping job. This way, if problems arise, you will be able to get them resolved effectively and efficiently.
- **Practice being detail oriented.** The more detailed you are, the happier your employer will be with your performance, which will benefit you in the long run. On your regular shop-

ping excursions, make a point of observing your surroundings, interactions with employees, the cleanliness of the store, and the friendliness of the cashier. When you do go on an actual assignment, you'll have a good basis for comparison and will be able to spot-check easily.

■ **Be aware of your local consumer laws.** Florida and Nevada both have laws regarding mystery shopping. Visit the Nevada legislature website (www.leg.state.nv.us) and the Florida Senate website (www.flsenate.gov) for their respective regulations. Even if you don't live in one of these states, it's a good idea to check your state's laws regarding fair consumer and retail practices to be sure that you abide by the relevant policies and regulations while you are conducting business as a mystery shopper.

Mystery shopping, when done in conjunction with the other income-generating ideas you have learned about, can provide you with the extra income you have been seeking to make ends meet, provide the creature comforts we all need periodically, or just allow you some monthly "fun money" to play with. No matter what you do with your earnings, mystery shopping is a fast-growing, lucrative enterprise that you will certainly want to jump into with both feet. In no time you will be earning money to shop and getting loads of free stuff, too!

Chapter 8

Auctions

Auction ('ok-shun): a process in which savvy shoppers bid for merchandise you no longer have an interest in maintaining

I had this really cool retro dress that I'd kept around for nostalgic reasons. With the new baby on the way, I had to make room and the dress had to go. So I eBayed it, and someone paid me $68! Imagine that!

—DONNA, *Kentucky*

Can I Really Make Money?

Are you ready to clean out that basement or closet? Tired of packing away things you will never use again? Good! We will teach you how to take your old junk and turn it into cold hard cash that you can take straight to the bank.

Who wants to spend hours going through their old things, pricing, and setting up for a garage sale only to find bargain hunters unwilling to pay fifty cents for an old scarf or run the risk of canceling on account of rain? Avoid the hassle, reach more people, and never get wet again.

While you may not get rich quick selling things on eBay, you would be amazed by the things people will buy in an online auction. These auctions reach millions of people daily, a much larger audience than you could ever hope to reach on your own. It is a sound way to supplement your income and rid yourself of items you no longer want or need. If you are extra-ambitious, you can use your bargain hunting savvy, craft skills, or even your passion for antiques to set up your own storefront in the online auction arena. The sky is the limit, whether it's a few extra pennies or a full-time income you're after, online auctioning may be your ticket.

The first step is to become familiar with the online auction sites suggested here and see just what people are selling. You may learn that those $15 shower curtains you passed up on your local store clearance shelf are selling for $50 to $60 on eBay to boutique clothing makers. Just when you thought something had no value, someone on eBay will surprise you.

If you build a positive reputation as an auctioneer and present your auctions in a smart, professional manner, you will have bidders and make money. We don't claim to have all the answers or top-secret tricks that will earn you a fortune, but we will provide you with basic commonsense advice and sound tips to help you get started.

Getting Started

While jumping into online auctioning may seem overwhelming, taking some time to understand the process will alleviate some of your concerns. Let's discuss the basics so you can become familiar with the inner workings of these sites.

■ **Registration.** Most auction sites require you to register in order to sell your merchandise through them. In most cases you will need to provide the following information: name, address, telephone number, and a valid e-mail address. You will also be asked to select a unique user ID and a password.

■ **Buying and selling.** Once you have registered, you can bid on any auction you choose, but often you must set up a seller's account before you can start earning money as an auction entrepreneur. To become a registered seller, you must generally provide the site with a credit or debit card, as well as your bank information. If you are uncomfortable with this arrangement, some auction websites offer alternatives such as providing substitute information for you. However, keep in mind that often this alternative requires that you pay a fee. Verifications are required for auction websites to provide a safe community within which to buy and sell items. It is essential for your protection. If you choose to work with established sites, providing this information is a safe and effective way to prove your identity.

I'm Ready to Sell!

You've completed registration as a buyer and a seller, so what's next? Once you are ready to sell, the procedure, while it may seem daunting, is really quite simple once you get the hang of it. The first thing on the agenda is choosing the selling format that is right for you. Here are a few well-known choices for formats you will want to familiarize yourself with.

■ **Classic online auction.** This is a standard auction in which the item is sold to the highest bidder. It is the most common format. You can offer bidding on one or multiple items in this format. Auctioning multiple items at the same time is generally referred to as a "Dutch auction." These auctions run one, three, five, seven, or ten days.

■ **Fixed price.** This option allows you as the auctioneer to set a price for your item with no bidding involved. You set a buy it now (BIN) price, and purchasers can choose to buy the item at your fixed price. As previously noted, there may be restrictions on using the BIN feature. Be sure to familiarize yourself with the auction website terms. You can sell single or multiple items in this format. Auctions run three, five, seven, or ten days.

■ **Auction stores.** Items can be purchased immediately, with no bidding, from your own electronic store setup. You must establish a store to use this format, and you may sell single or multiple items. Typical auctions run one, two, three, or four months.

Remember, online auctions are a business, and fees will apply when listing items for sale. Check with each website to determine what your fees will be and how they must be paid. This information should be readily available in the website's FAQ section.

Planning and Managing Your Auctions

Now that you have a basic understanding of the auction process, let's take a more in-depth look at the details and how to best sell your items.

Auction Start and End Times

How do you know when to start and end your auction? This all depends on the length of the auction. You will want it to end at a peak bidding time. This is usually in the evening and on a weekend, when most people have the time to monitor an auction of an item they want. If you choose a seven-day auction, it may be best to start it on Monday sometime in the early evening, as it will end at the same time the following Sunday, or Monday, depending on the auction site calculations. This should offer most people an opportunity to see your items and follow your auction. Try to avoid ending your auctions on holidays, as most people will be busy and not using their computers to shop online. Also, keep in mind that many people are not on their personal computers during their prime-time television shows. Avoid ending your auctions at these key times and it may provide you with better bidding results. Several websites, such as Auction Bytes (www.auctionbytes.com), offer auction forecasts. While these are not 100 percent proven methods, there are some good tips and suggestions to be found.

Select a Category

You will also have to choose which category to list your items in, such as books, baby clothing, maternity, and so forth. Researching the categories other auctioneers have had success with is one of the best ways to get started. Search for similar items and make a note of the categories they are listed under. There are many categories to choose from, so select wisely. You will want your item to be easily accessible to "auction browsers;" people who window-shop auction sites with a specific category in mind, if not a specific item. Good placement can help you find impulse buyers on the Internet.

Choose a Title

This is also a very important part of your auction. Your title is what will bring people to your auction searching for a specific item. For example, you will want to title it with as much specific information as possible. It is good to list the brand name, size, if it is new with tags (NWT), and other information you feel is pertinent to your auction. Your title could look something like this: "Girls Mudd Jeans Size 6X/NWT."

If a bidder searches for "new Mudd Jeans size 6," your auction is a perfect match, so your title will lead the bidder right to you. Often it is all in the wording. In this fast-paced world, some people don't have the time to look through multiple listings. Giving as much detail as allowable in the title streamlines the process for your bidders and makes it easier for them to quickly determine their interest level in your auction.

Be sure to use acronyms in order to fit the maximum keywords into your auction title. Some common acronyms used in auction titles are as follows:

- **NWT**   New with tags
- **NWOT**   New without tags
- **MIB**   Mint in box
- **NEW**   Brand-new condition
- **XS**   Extra small
- **SM**   Small
- **MD**   Medium
- **LG**   Large
- **XL**   Extra large
- **XXL**   Double extra large
- **XXXL**   Triple extra large
- **SZ**   Size

Browse through the auction website you are working with for lists of additional acronyms that may be helpful for use in your item titles.

Provide Pictures

As the old saying goes, "A picture is worth a thousand words." This analogy could not hold any truer than it does in an online auction. People want to see what you are selling. You can describe the item in such detail that an average reader can envision it with incredible accuracy within their own mind, but the bottom line is, if they can see it, it will encourage their bid. Take good-quality pictures of your products with a digital camera, or scan the pictures in from traditional film and your chances of selling them will increase tenfold. Several pictures from different perspectives work best. Sticking with our jeans example, you will want to take pictures of the front and back of the jeans, as well as a close-up of the brand name. People like to know up front they are getting what they pay for.

If you don't own a digital camera or scanner, check with friends and family to see if you might borrow one for your auction items, or consider purchasing one. Simple digital devices may be purchased for as little as $20, and a more sophisticated camera may run upward of $100. Determine what will work best for you based on your needs. Many of the simple cameras work wonderfully and will offer a decent quality picture for your auction needs.

Set a Starting Price

If you are wondering what price to start your auction at, you can research similar items and see what starting prices other auctioneers have had the best luck with. We would recommend selecting a low starting price to stimulate bids on your auction. People like to think they have a chance at snagging an item for a rock-bottom price. If you start your auction too high, interest may be diminished.

Some auctions allow you to set a reserve price for your item. This is a set amount, undisclosed to the bidder, which is the minimum price your merchandise will sell for. This is usually not required for small items, like individual articles of clothing, but you may want to consider it if you have an item of exceptional value, such as a collectable or an antique. If your reserve price is not met, you are not obligated to sell the item and can try again.

You also may have the opportunity to set a buy it now price for your auction. This is a flat price the buyer can use to purchase the item. As a general rule, BIN can only be used by a purchaser before any bids have been made for the auction.

Provide a Good Item Description

A good item description is another important aspect of online auctioning. You will want to offer detailed information about the item you are selling. Research similar items and read their descriptions. Base yours on the auctions you would be most likely to bid on as a buyer. Information that you will want in your description should include, but not be limited to, the following:

- Color and texture
- Item size and/or dimensions
- Brand or maker
- Age of item
- Condition of item
- Features that make your item unique

You will want to try to anticipate any questions that may arise from a possible buyer and include answers in your description. An exceptionally detailed description will help fend off the potential e-mail onslaught a poorly described item can present.

Keep it honest. If your item is damaged in any way, you will want to be certain to describe the damage in great detail, as well as provide clear photos of the imperfections. Be sure your bidders know exactly what they are bidding on. This includes normal wear and tear as well. While normal pilling or fading on clothing may not be a big deal to you, it may be a big deal to your buyer, and you want each and every buyer to be 100 percent satisfied with his or her transaction.

Consider Shipping Methods

Another choice you will have to make is how you want to ship your auction items. The main forms of shipping within the United States are the United States Postal Service (USPS), UPS, or FedEx. Things to consider when choosing a shipping agent are weight, size, time to delivery, and convenience to you. The post office and UPS allow you to print shipping labels right from your PC, though you may find FedEx to be less expensive for heavier or bulky items, and they may be cheaper for individuals (as opposed to companies) depending on delivery zone. You will have to see what types of items you will be selling and visit the shipping companies' websites to decide which method is best for you. You may choose one and stick with it, or you may vary from one method to another. Sometimes auctioneers even let their buyers choose a shipping method. It's all about finding what works best for you.

You will also need to decide where you are willing to ship. Will it be the continental United States only? Will you include Canada? Or are you willing to ship worldwide? Overseas shipping rates are usually much higher, and shipping to a foreign country can sometimes prove difficult, depending on the item being shipped. If you choose to ship to the United States only, be sure to state this clearly in your auction to prevent unwanted bids and unhappy customers.

Get a feel for preferred shipping methods by researching auctions similar to yours. We cannot stress enough how important it is to know your market.

Visit these sites for more information on shipping:

- United States Postal Service (www.usps.com)
- FedEx (www.fedex.com)
- UPS (www.ups.com)
- DHL (www.dhl-usa.com)

Determining Shipping and Handling Costs

This is a slippery slope among the online auction community. Our advice is to keep your shipping estimate as close to the actual cost as possible. Auction participants frown on padded shipping charges, and if it is padded excessively, it may be against the website's fair practice rules. It is not unusual to increase shipping slightly to cover shipping and packing supplies, as well as your time, but it must be within reason. Research similar items to get a feel for what items cost to ship; use the shipping resources listed to help determine price; and if you include a handling fee, be sure to state that clearly in your auctions. If you accidentally overcharge someone by a substantial amount, we recommend you consider refunding a portion of the shipping, as this is good business and will help you build a positive reputation within the community.

The option for delivery confirmation, as well as insurance, should be included in shipping and handling. You can make both of these mandatory or optional for the bidder. We strongly recommend encouraging your bidders to take both, as it is generally an inexpensive way for both buyer and seller to be protected. Be sure to charge the actual cost for these services, and state clearly whether they are optional or required.

Payment

What forms of payment will you accept as a seller? It is very important that you spell out your terms of payment clearly and concisely. Here is a list of some available options and the benefits of each.

■ **PayPal.** You can receive funds from a verified bank account or credit card. This is an immediate and convenient form of traceable payment, and it offers protection for both seller and buyer. It is deposited directly into your account.

■ **Personal or cashier checks.** You receive funds from a person's personal bank account via USPS. You will probably want to wait until a personal check clears before shipping the item. Be sure to spell this out in your payment terms to avoid confusion for your bidders.

■ **Money orders.** Another form of payment received via USPS, money orders are a safe bet because the buyer has to pay for the money order with cash before sending it as payment. You may wish to wait for payment to clear before shipping. Remember to state this in your payment terms.

■ **Escrow.** Monies are held in escrow by a third party until the transaction is completed. Be sure to use a reputable service, as there are many fraudulent escrow companies out there, and you will want to protect yourself as best you can. This form of payment is generally only used in high-value auctions, such as for vehicles, where the value of the auction is over $500. A good resource is to check with individual auction websites for recommendations on escrow companies.

■ **Bank-to-bank wire transfers.** Payment is sent from the buyer's bank to yours. It is immediate and convenient but offers little protection for the buyer. It is not easy to recover funds in case of fraud. If you choose to offer this option to your buyers, you should also offer your contact information so the buyer can be sure your information is accurate and can be validated.

■ **Concealed cash.** Payment is sent by mail or package carrier in the form of currency. (Typically dollars and change wrappers in a sheet of paper or concealed in some other manner.) This option is not recommended but is still offered by some auctioneers. There is little protection for the buyer, and it is unlikely that savvy shoppers would be willing to risk their hard-earned money on this payment method. Nevertheless, it is an option, so we decided to include it.

When laying out your terms of payment, you will want to let the buyer know when you expect to receive payment in clear, respectful terms. You will want to include something like "Payment expected within five days of the auction's end. Failure to pay will result in relisting of the item, and you will be reported as a nonpaying bidder."

Be careful to avoid using terms like "no exceptions," as this is the real world and legitimate things can happen to otherwise honest people that prevent them from meeting your demands. Once you have spelled out your terms, you have recourse should someone not pay, but take each situation on a case-by-case basis.

By having clearly defined auction terms, you will avoid a lot of problems at payment time. Refer to other auctioneers' terms as a guide to determine what will work best for you.

Stay Organized

Staying organized before and after the close of your auctions can be the difference between a smooth transaction and a botched deal. Keep a close eye on your auctions, and be prepared to answer bidders' questions in a timely fashion. Use the tools provided by the auction site to be sure you do not miss out on any bids because you were unable to respond to an inquiry. Be sure to keep your packages and addresses straight, especially when you have multiple auctions open at the same time. Sending the wrong packages to winning bidders can be a costly error for you, as you would be forced to pay return shipping fees or fees for your winners to send the package to the appropriate party. Keep a log or journal detailing who gets what, as well as when you shipped the items.

Additional Auction Tips

Depending on which items you choose to sell via auction, the following information may come in handy and help add more dollars to your bottom line.

■ **Packaging.** Be sure to package your items in a professional way. If the item is fragile and breakable, an investment in some bubble wrap will save you the aggravation of a buyer complaint that the item was improperly packed and arrived broken. Save your old newspapers as well; they make excellent filler for boxes.

■ **Clothing.** Think about selling your clothing in small lots of similar items. Offering two or three outfits rather than a single item is often more appealing to a bidder. This will also make shipping more convenient for you as you will not need to pack each item individually.

■ **Multiple wins.** If you have a bidder who wins multiple auctions, consider combining shipping for them. Maximizing your bidders' savings will keep them coming back for more.

■ **Add pizzazz.** Once you have the basics down pat, many auction sites offer the ability to add backgrounds, colors, and even music to your auctions. You will want to look at using additional photos to enhance your offerings, as well as the other ways you can help your auction stand out in a crowd. Some of these options come with a fee attached; you will want to check with the individual sites to see what types of "bells and whistles" they offer to give your auctions that added punch. Make sure to check how much they cost before adding them, too.

■ **Stick with the biggies.** These sites generally offer some sort of protection for their users and have been tested by time. If you are bold enough to try a lesser known site, be sure to read through all of the information available about it before you get involved. You will want to know what the site will do for you should you encounter a substantial problem with a bidder. Here are a few auction websites with an established Internet presence:

- MSN Auctions (www.auctions.msn.com)
- eBay (www.ebay.com)
- Yahoo Auctions (www.auctions.yahoo.com)
- Amazon Auctions (www.auctions.amazon.com)
- Goodwill (www.shopgoodwill.com). For buying only.
- UBID (www.ubid.com)
- Overstock (www.auctions.overstock.com)

- **Have fun!** Using your creative writing skills is definitely a way to draw traffic to your auction. Just be sure you remain within the terms of use for the auction site you have chosen, and watch your hit counter and bids climb when you add a little flair to your listing.

Feedback: Your Online Reputation

What is feedback? It is a brief description of how a transaction went between yourself and another online auction site member. It is left by both buyer and seller, and it can tell you a lot about the people you encounter in the community.

Reputation is a crucial part of the online auctioning community. It allows potential bidders to look at your past transactions in order to get a feel for how you interact within the community. It allows them to see your positive transactions as well as your transgressions, so they are able to form an educated opinion of your credibility and have the confidence to bid or the ability to pass on your auctions.

How do you establish a positive reputation in the world of online auctions? The easiest way to start building feedback is to become a buyer. If you bid on an auction and pay immediately, you have upheld your half of the bargain, and positive feedback should be left for you at that time. Unfortunately, many sellers wait until you leave feedback for them, their fear being the potential negative you "could" leave them and their lack of recourse. If you conduct yourself in a professional manner and handle your auction to the best of your ability, negative feedback will not be a concern. In these cases, once the transaction is completed smoothly, you can be sure appropriate feedback will be left, as everyone in the auction community knows its importance.

If you choose to begin selling without any feedback, here are some things you will want to do to ensure positive comments are left:

■ **Communicate.** Good communication is crucial to a positive auction experience. If your auction winner e-mails you with a question about shipping or payment, you should offer a prompt response to their inquiry. When people are left hanging, they tend to get nervous, and the last thing you want is a nervous buyer.

■ **Stay up-to-date.** Be sure to update your contact information as needed with the online auction websites you use. Keeping your personal information updated is important in case the auction website or a bidder needs to contact you with a question. Don't miss a sale opportunity by not having accurate information in your profile.

■ **Ship in a timely fashion.** Once payment has been made, any delay in shipping may reflect badly on you. While establishing your reputation, speedy shipping will always bode well with your buyers.

■ **Resolve conflicts.** Don't be overly stubborn if a bidder informs you he or she is unhappy with the item purchased. There will always be people in this world who are dissatisfied. Try to resolve the situation amicably, and avoid negative feedback. Most bidders want to rectify the situation as well, with as little hassle as possible. You could offer a partial refund or allow the bidder to return the item, at his or her expense, for a full refund. The minimal money lost in fees is not worth tarnishing your reputation.

■ **Leave feedback.** If your winning bidder meets the terms of your auction, make sure to leave appropriate feedback for them immediately. This is a good-faith offering that shows your buyer your intentions for a smooth transaction are true.

Following these guidelines will make you a shining star in the auction community of your choice in no time. Once members know you are a trusted seller, they will be much more likely to take a chance on one of your auctions, which only stands to increase the profits on your merchandise.

Potential Pitfalls

As with every other aspect of the Internet, auctions are not
without dangers. While problems don't occur with tremendous
frequency, in such large communities you are bound to have
a few rotten apples.

Things to look out for as both buyer and seller include the
following.

Nonpaying Bidders

Some people view online auctions as a joke and will bid on
your auctions with no intention of paying, if this happens,
attempt to rectify the situation through e-mail, but if your bidder does not pay, check with the site hosting your auction to
see what you can do and leave appropriate feedback for the
buyer. Most auction sites allow you to file what is known as a
"nonpaying bidder" report, and they allow you to relist the
item at no cost.

While managing your in-progress auctions, you have the
right to choose who bids on your auctions and who does not.
You can refuse any bids from buyers with excessive negative
feedback or no feedback at all. Be careful when dealing with
newbies; don't reject them immediately. Most are honest, legitimate bidders, and everyone has to start somewhere. Ease your
mind by e-mailing the bidder to ensure he or she intends to
pay. Newbies can become your best customers.

Difficult Winners

If a winner e-mails you after receiving an item stating it is broken or otherwise damaged, you have a right as the seller to
request proof of the damage. Do not take everyone you
encounter at their word. There are people out there who will
attempt to take advantage of a new seller by making fraudu-

lent claims on an item's condition. These people are generally looking for a partial refund and want to keep the item. If you know it was packed securely, demand proof before offering any resolution, or suggest that the buyer return the item to you prior to your issuing a refund.

Shill Bidders

Shill bidding is fraudulent bidding on an item intended to drive up the price of the auction. This is not allowed on the big auction sites, and though difficult to prove, it is not impossible. If you suspect shill bidding is occurring on an auction you are looking at, check the seller's other items and see if the same user is bidding on those. This is a technique often used by unsavory auctioneers. Report such behavior to the site handling the auction, and they will take appropriate action.

Nonshipping Seller

If you have won an auction but have not received the item in a reasonable amount of time, you may be dealing with an auction swindler. Hopefully you paid using a method offering protection, and you will have recourse in recovering your money. Notify your payment source as well as the site hosting the auction and allow them to deal directly with the seller.

Note: If you are using PayPal, you only have a limited amount of time to file a claim on an item that's not received. Be sure to read their policies thoroughly so you understand your rights as a buyer.

We hope that any experiences you have with online auctions are fun and problem-free. Should you encounter a problem, following the policies of the organizations you chose to deal with should end with an agreeable resolution. When you are in the right, stick to your guns and be persistent; remember, the squeakiest wheel gets the oil. Happy auctioning!

Chapter 9
Swapping and Sales

Sell ('sel): the art of persuading someone to take merchandise off your hands for monetary gain
Trade: ('trAd): the art of exchanging merchandise so
 that both parties benefit equally.

*M*y daughter desperately wanted the black Lab
 McDonald's was offering during one of their pro-
*motions. I was able to trade a miniature schnauzer for the
Lab with another member of my favorite parenting board.
Both of our girls were just thrilled.*

—MEG, *Minnesota*

Why Swap?

Looking for an alternative to auctions to find a home for excess
merchandise, crafts, or garage-sale items? You may consider
selling or swapping your stuff online with your fellow com-

munity members. Swapping on the Internet is becoming the
way to barter in the new millennium. You will find people
swapping everything from coupons and gift cards to Happy
Meal toys and games. Someone out there wants what you have
and may very well have what you want.

Swapping on the Internet can be very beneficial. Expenses
are minimal and gains are maximized. For example, you have
a bag full of baby clothing in good condition taking up valuable space in your closet. Even though your daughter has out-
grown them, you are hanging on to them "just in case." Your
eighteen-month-old son is growing by leaps and bounds, and
you just spent a small fortune on a wardrobe for him that he
seemed to outgrow the next day. Maybe there is a mom in a
similar position who would be willing to trade clothing. She
has the toddler boy 2Ts you need, and you have the baby girl
items she needs. It's an ideal situation—you both get the items
you need with minimal out-of-pocket expenses.

Instead of swapping, you may choose to sell your items.
This may not be as profitable as an online auction, but it is not
without merit, as there are no fees involved. As a general rule,
members of deal or freebie boards are looking for an awesome
bargain and will rarely consider purchasing items that may be
overpriced. You will want to let potential buyers know the
price you would like to receive as well as shipping costs.

Swap Till You Drop

There are so many things that you can trade online; it is often
surprising to see what people are offering. Look at some of the
more popular items you may wish to consider trading.

■ **Coupons.** After learning about couponing in Chapter 4, you may now have an abundance of extra coupons that
you do not use. Why not arrange to swap them with another

online user or friend for coupons you can use. Start by finding out what types of coupons others are interested in and giving them your wish list in return. If you both have coupons
that match each other's need—make a swap. These don't need
to be exact face dollar value on the coupon trades. If you both
receive additional savings, then you both win. Try your best
to match savings, but keep in mind that if the coupon has no
value to you, it is always better to share it and receive coupons
that do put money back in your pocket.

- **Video games, movies, music, and books.** Do you
have piles of games no one is playing? Does your closet already
look like a library, and you are looking for more books to read?
Have you watched your collection of movies one time too
many? Then consider trading them for something new with an
online member or a friend in a similar predicament. Swap a
game for a game, a movie for a movie, and so on. You'll both
have new entertainment for very little cost.

- **Clothing.** Trade unwanted clothing for items you can
use. Whether it is for you or a family member, you'll find your
wardrobe options expanding.

- **Fast-food toys.** Trying to complete that set of mini
Beanie Babies? Does your son or daughter really want that last
character from their favorite new movie, but you just couldn't
get it? Someone online probably has an extra and may be willing to trade with you.

- **Gift certificates.** While no gifts are without merit, you
know you will never use that gift certificate Aunt Rose gave
you for a new restaurant because you don't like Italian and
that's their main fare. Someone else may have a gift certificate
for a national retailer that you shop at regularly but he or she
will never visit. Trade them, and you will both win in the end.

- **Crafts.** Do you make beautiful quilts but wish you
could knit mittens and scarves? Consider swapping your tal-
ents with other crafters. Perhaps you could quilt a comforter
for their child and they could make mittens and scarves for

you and your crew. As long as the material cost is comparable, you will have a wonderful handcrafted exchange.

■ **Products and services.** Perhaps you have a home-based business selling kitchen goods and you are in dire need of business cards. There may be an online user or friend who has relatives in or owns a print shop. You may be able to swap that fancy kitchen gadget he or she wants for your much-needed box of business cards. Typically these arrangements wind up saving money on both ends as you'll both be able to use your wholesale discounts to obtain items you might have to pay twice as much for otherwise.

The sky is the limit when trading online, so be creative. Let people know what you are looking for and what you have to offer. If you can't find a swapping partner, you can always offer your items for sale.

Show Me the Money

When you decide to sell your items online without the aid of an auction website, you will need to consider what forms of payment you will accept. The available methods of payment are similar to those accepted on the auction sites. Here are a few to consider:

■ **PayPal.** You will typically receive the funds immediately in your online account.

■ **Personal check.** Be sure to let your buyer know that you reserve the right to ship the item after the check has cleared. You may decide not to delay shipping if it is someone you already have an established relationship with, but you may want to proceed with more caution when dealing with someone new. Use your best judgment.

■ **Money order.** As with a personal check, you may wish to cash the money order before shipping the merchandise.

These payment methods will work adequately for swapping costs as well. When swapping, you will simply pay the costs to ship your own items, and the member you are swapping with will cover their shipping charges. In most swaps, no other money changes hands. Occasionally, you may make a trade that benefits one member over the other. In this case, you can request or offer a payment to balance the scales.

Swapping and Selling Successfully

Follow these tips to help ensure a smooth transaction when swapping or selling online.

- **Set a fair and reasonable price.** You need to be realistic when pricing items for sale online. You can set your expectations lower with a private sale because you will incur no fees. Think about how much you would realistically be willing to pay for the item if it were offered to you. Then try to offer your prospective buyers a deal they can't refuse. You will be more likely to sell your merchandise quickly this way, resulting in money in your pocket. If you are completely unsure what a fair price is, ask your online buddies or friends what they would be willing to pay for your item. They will offer fair and honest feedback, and they may even want to buy it from you.
- **Honesty is really the best policy.** Be sure to describe your items honestly. If there are defects or problems, you will want your buyer to know before the sale, not after. Offer pictures, if possible, and detailed descriptions to ensure there are no misunderstandings.
- **Know the member.** It would be prudent to conduct online sales and trades with members you already have a relationship with. Since you do not have the same recourse you have in an auction, you have to be very careful who you deal with. Sticking with people you trust is sound advice.

■ **Do your part.** Be sure you are able to follow through on your end. Set a shipping date with your swapper and stick to it. Communicate with your buyer throughout the process to ensure a clear understanding.

■ **Ask for feedback.** While it's not as formal as the feedback you find on auction websites, most forums that allow swapping have a section for "bad" traders or sellers. Be sure to check this information before initiating a trade or sale with anyone you are unsure of. After you successfully trade or sell an item to members, ask them to leave you a good reference, and be sure to do the same for them.

■ **Get the word out.** Regardless of how your transaction went, let others know. If you had a smooth transaction with a member, informing your community will make people more willing to deal with you and the other member. Obviously a bad transaction should be noted prominently within your forum. No sense in allowing anyone else to be hurt by a bad trader, seller, or buyer.

Swap and Shop

There are communities on the Internet that are solely dedicated to selling and swapping your merchandise. Be sure to check with your favorite online communities. Many online boards have special sections dedicated to trades and sales. While they offer this option to their users as a convenience, they will hold no responsibility for a sale or trade gone sour.

Here are a few selling websites to get you started:

■ Barnes & Noble (www.barnesandnoble.com/frames/ selltextbooks). Have old college textbooks lying around? This book retailer offers an option for you to sell your used books.

■ Amazon.com (www.amazon.com). Amazon offers you the option of selling your new and used items on their website provided they carry the particular item. Note that Amazon does charge fees if you sell an item. Listing your item, however, is free. In addition, your transactions are monitored by Amazon, which provides a higher level of secure and successful transactions.

■ Café Press (www.cafepress.com). Are you an artist? In need of a creative fund-raiser for your organization? Do you have a great idea for a T-shirt or mug? How about a demo CD you'd like to put up for sale? Try Café Press's options for a no-cost way to produce your items and set up a virtual shop for sales.

■ Trader Online (www.traderonline.com). Do you have something bigger to sell or trade such as a car, mobile home, boat, or piece of farm equipment? This site offers free Internet listing, and for a modest fee, you can also list your classified in *Auto Trader* or other appropriate regional magazines offered.

Here are a few of our favorite swapping websites:

■ Blossom Swap (www.blossomswap.com). Gardeners galore swap information, seeds, ideas, and other gardening-related things.

■ My Coupons (www.mycoupons.com). This website includes a fast-paced coupon swapping forum for advanced traders (may be a little intimidating for newcomers).

■ Title Trader (www.titletrader.com). This website was established for online trading of books, DVDs, and CDs.

■ Swap and Save (www.swapandsave.com). This site offers a Swap Central area where you will find all types of items available for trade.

While setting up to swap, you may also choose to take advantage of the free web hosting available or special websites that allow you storage areas for your swapping needs. Most sites are fairly easy to use and will offer you templates and step-by-step instructions to help you get started. Here are some popular storage websites:

- Photo Bucket (www.photobucket.com). Photo storage.
- Shutterfly (www.shutterfly.com). Photo storage.
- Yahoo GeoCities (www.geocities.yahoo.com). Web page builders, hosting, and e-mail services.
- Angelfire (www.angelfire.lycos.com). Web page builders, hosting, and e-mail services.

Note that these sites are subject to advertisements in return for providing you with tools and storage for hosting your website. Be sure to read each site's terms of service, and know the rules and guidelines for using the site before investing your time and energy creating a web page. Often free pages may not be used for profit ventures.

Also, consider your own Internet service provider's options. Providers generally give you web space or a home page for as long as you subscribe to their service.

Risky Business

Unfortunately, there are a few risks involved in swapping or selling online. As we pointed out earlier, not everyone on the Internet is an upstanding community member. This does not mean you should shy away from selling or swapping online; it just means you should use caution and your instincts before you involve yourself in any online deal.

As a seller, you will minimize your risks by being clear when stating your terms for sale and deciding to hold shipments until payment has been received and cleared. The worst consequence you may face by practicing these habits is the possibility of having to find another potential buyer because the original buyer doesn't want to adhere to your terms.

As a buyer, you run the risk of sending payment and not receiving the item you purchased. One way to diminish your risk is to use a credit card or PayPal whenever possible, as you will have more recourse in the event that a seller does not come through.

When swapping, the best advice we can give you is to swap with members of a board you know or those who have a proven track record of swapping successfully with others. This is not a guarantee that your transaction will go smoothly, but it does increase the odds of a positive experience.

When trading or selling online using your own web space or online communities, there is not much recourse when a transaction does not go according to plan. If a bad trade happens to you, contact the website owner and have the trader listed on any bad seller/trader lists available; have the website owner address the individual if possible. At the very least, it is important to take the steps necessary to have any negative experiences documented with the board's owner. You may wind up with a more positive resolution, or you may at least have confidence that the individual will not upset other members with his or her bad trading practices.

With that said, it is important to remember that most transactions will go smoothly and will be a positive experience for all involved. While there may always be a bad banana or two in the bunch, the majority of online users are good honest people, just like you!

Chapter 10

Peer Networking

Forum ('fOr-ahm): an online neighborhood that allows you to gain knowledge and make friends on the information superhighway

Being a mom of four makes it difficult to get together with my "real-life" friends. My online friendships have gotten me through so much; I'm not sure what I would do without them.

—Susan, *California*

Now that you have mastered all the basics in this book, you may be wondering where to go from here. The resources of the Internet are endless, and peer-to-peer networking is an invaluable part of the Internet experience. With an infinite variety of message boards in existence and new ones forming every day, you will never be at a loss to find someone who has the information you seek.

What Is a Forum?

Forums are the cork bulletin boards of the Internet. They are a place to leave messages and questions about a particular topic, as well as receive responses that are informative and candid from a wide variety of people. Unlike e-mail, you are not reaching just one individual, but rather an entire community of people.

The number of forum boards that exist is virtually infinite. For example, there are forums for parenting, freebies, science fiction fans, and book lovers, just to name a few. Whatever your interest, if others share it, you are likely to find several forums dedicated to the topic.

Finding the forum that works best for you is a trial-and-error process. Through use, you will feel at home with the format of your choice in no time at all.

Content and community are the most important factors to consider when joining a forum. If it has the information you are looking for and the members seem friendly and welcoming, adjusting to the format will be a breeze.

Where Are These Forums?

Finding topic-specific forums is a simple process. Use your search engine by typing in the keywords that are likely to lead you in the right direction. For example, find freebie or deals boards by typing phrases such as "freebie forums," "freebie message boards," or "Internet deals message boards" into the search engine.

While Internet message boards come and go, here's a starter list of freebie and bargain hunting–related forums:

- Fat Wallet (www.fatwallet.com)
- Fishing for Deals (www.fishingfordeals.com)

- iVillage (www.ivillage.com)
- My Coupons (www.mycoupons.com)

What's the Right Place for Me?

A good way to get a feel for an online community is to "lurk" on the board before jumping in and joining the fun. Lurking means to read the board's postings without participating directly in the conversation. Some boards move fast, with many new postings each day. Others are slower and may only have a few postings a day or several days with no activity. You will find that some boards are all business and only have threads referring to the topic at hand; others have areas on the board for off-topic chitchat. Again, what works for you will all boil down to your personal preference. Taking some time to understand the boards you are interested in will make your decision to join or move on to something different a lot easier.

Joining a board and becoming an active member may seem like an overwhelming proposition at first, but you will find that most community members are open to welcoming new people and fresh perspectives to the boards.

The following is a breakdown of the different requirements you may encounter when deciding to join a community.

■ **Forums that require registration.** Perhaps the most common forum you will encounter is the one that requires you to choose a user ID and password before you can participate in board activities. It will be necessary for you to log into your account each time you visit the board if you wish to join the conversation. This is done so the board owner or administrator can keep track of the people posting on the forum.

■ **Forums that require you to apply for membership.** Some forum owners require that you apply for membership before you can even read the messages posted on the board. Generally, the application is painless; you simply register for an account with the administrator, click the Apply for Membership button, and await a response from the administrator of the board. This is usually done in tight-knit communities that want active board members rather than lurkers from the get-go.

- **Forums that have no requirements to post.** Boards requiring nothing special to participate are becoming a dying breed on the Internet. They offer little security to the members and allow a poster to misrepresent themselves or use a false identity. These boards are definitely the minority, but they do still exist.

Are There Negatives to Participating on a Message Board?

Generally, the Internet community experience is a pleasant one, but there are some snafus you may encounter while posting. Do not let them deter you from finding your niche; when you take the time to check out the various boards available, you are sure to find one that fits you perfectly.

In larger communities, you may find the existing members less than receptive to newbies. They seem to have little patience for someone just learning the ropes and are often not afraid to say so. They may get irritated if you post a freebie that has already been posted or start a thread in the wrong place. Do not let these people scare you off. You are just learning the ins and outs of forum posting, and you will get the hang of it.

However, if you find the active members of a particular forum too harsh, you can always continue to lurk and gain knowledge, and then move on to friendlier communities in which to take part.

Also, acknowledge the fact that you are on the Internet, and while you may start to feel like you know the people you are posting with, they are still strangers. You really have no way of knowing whether they are who they profess to be. There are a few people who will use the anonymous nature of the Web to create a false identity.

In general, this is absolutely harmless, but there are people who prey on unsuspecting, generous online communities. Be sure to read Chapters 11 and 12 for more information on pitfalls, scams, and spam.

Netiquette, in Short

A critical part of being understood on the Internet is to practice the basics of netiquette with every encounter you have. The word, itself, is simply a shortened version of "net etiquette," but the meaning goes much further. It is a series of rules or guidelines that makes each and every Internet user's experience better.

Clearly defined guidelines help all societies, even virtual ones. While you don't stand to face fifty lashes with a wet noodle for not following the guidelines put forth in this chapter, you may wind up in the virtual hot seat if you do not. You can potentially be banned from online communities by not practicing good netiquette.

First, it is good practice to introduce yourself to existing board members when you decide to join an established forum. It lets the existing members know that you are ready to be a part of the forum and, at the same time, they get a feel for your posting style and personality.

Second, familiarize yourself with the style of the forum. Often things such as typing in all capital letters is a forum no-no. Using all capitals is the equivalent to yelling, so if you don't want to shout, keep the Caps Lock off.

As you become more familiar with online message boards, you will notice a lot of posts contain a type of shorthand using acronyms. Here is a list of the most popular ones in use to help you understand just what you are reading:

- **.02**   My two cents worth
- **BIL**   Brother-in-law
- **B&M**   Brick and mortar, retail store
- **BTDT**   Been there, done that
- **CYE**   See your e-mail
- **DD**   Dear daughter
- **DH**   Dear husband
- **DS**   Dear son
- **DW**   Dear wife
- **FAQ**   Frequently asked questions
- **FIL**   Father-in-law
- **FWIW**   For what it's worth
- **FYI**   For your information
- ***G***   Grin
- **GCs**   Gift cards/certificates
- **GMTA**   Great minds think alike
- **HTH**   Hope this helps
- **IMBO**   In my biased opinion
- **IMHO**   In my humble opinion
- **IMO**   In my opinion
- **IOW**   In other words
- **IRL**   In real life
- **ISO**   In search of
- **J/K**   Joking
- **JMHO**   Just my humble opinion
- **KWIM**   Know what I mean
- **LMK**   Let me know
- **LOL**   Laughing out loud
- **M**   Message
- **MIL**   Mother-in-law
- **MSG**   Message

- **MTCW**   My two cents worth
- **MYOB**   Mind your own business
- **NAZ**   Name, address, zip code
- **NBD**   No big deal
- **NT**   No text
- **OMG**   Oh, my gosh
- **OTC**   Over-the-counter
- **OTOH**   On the other hand
- **PG**   Pregnant *or* playgroup
- **PITB**   Pain in the butt
- **POP**   Proof of purchase
- **POV**   Point of view
- **RAOK**   Random act of kindness
- **ROFL**   Rolling on floor laughing
- **ROTFLMBO**   Rolling on the floor laughing my butt off
- ***S***   Smile
- **SAHM**   Stay-at-home mom
- **SASE**   Self-addressed, stamped envelope
- **SIL**   Sister-in-law
- **TGIF**   Thank God it's Friday
- **TIA**   Thanks in advance
- **TIC**   Tongue in cheek
- **TTFN**   Ta-ta for now
- ***W***   Wink
- **WAHM**   Work-at-home mom
- **WOHM**   Work-outside-of-home mom
- **WWYD**   What would you do?
- **YMMV**   Your mileage may vary

Visit our website for a more in-depth look at message board etiquette as well as more information on how to post successfully in any Internet arena. We have set up a bulletin board of our own as a place for you to get your feet wet, and we would be happy to answer any questions you may have about posting.

Be sure to take the time to read each forum's FAQs and their privacy policies before joining to gain a fuller understanding of what the board's mission is. We hope that you will make visiting these communities part of your daily routine and can gain as much from them as we have. As they say on the Web, "See you on the boards!"

Chapter 11
Avoiding Pitfalls

Scam ('skam): a deceptive act by a sneaky company
or Internet user

*The first time I saw the Nigerian bank account scam,
I was shocked. I couldn't believe people would give
such sensitive and personal information out to a complete
stranger. The sad thing is that people are taken by scams
each and every day. . . .*

—Lisa, *California*

How to Spot a Scam

You have followed each lesson in this book and are well on
your way to making money, taking advantage of deals, and
finding the free stuff when *bam*! You are hit with a scam. How
do you tell? How do you spot a bad deal or a veiled get-rich-
quick scheme? It's all in knowing what to look for and being
aware of what to avoid.

While there are many fraudulent offers on the Web, if you follow these simple guidelines, you will be certain to stave off the majority of scams you encounter.

- **Trust your gut instinct.** If you do not feel comfortable or a deal appears too good to be true, chances are it is. Take heed of your skepticism and move on.
- **It's highly unlikely that you will get rich quick.** An offer promising to make you rich overnight is a sure sign of a scam. Run away! Certainly, there are people in the world who have obtained instant wealth, but odds are no person or company is going to make you wealthy beyond your wildest dreams just because you happened to stumble on their website. Watch for phrases like:

  - From welfare to millionaire in just a few days!
  - All you have to do is sign up. We do the rest, you collect the dollars.
  - Act now! One-time-only offer.
  - Last chance on this multimillion-dollar opportunity!

- **Be leery of a lack of support.** Beware of websites that do not offer customer service support or contact information readily. A legitimate business will always have support available on its website. You should not have to look far to find out who is sponsoring the offer and how to contact them. Customer support and contact information links are easy to find on bona fide websites. At a bare minimum, you will find a name and e-mail address listed to address any questions or offer the support you may need.
- **Guard your card.** Be cautious when entering credit card information to purchase items through a website. Before entering your information anywhere on the Internet, be certain that the website you are shopping offers a secure connec-

tion through which to make your purchase. A secure server simply scrambles or encrypts the information you enter, making it harder for a hacker or scam artist to obtain and make use of your submission.

An easy way to tell whether the retailer is using a secure server is to check the URL during the checkout process. Normally, you will see *http://* at the beginning of a website URL address. When the same web address becomes "secure," the URL will change to read *https://* at the beginning of the address. The *S* indicates that the web address is secure. If you do not see the *S* appear in this way—stop! You may be safer to call the business and make your purchase over the phone or move on to another company that does offer a secure checkout process.

Identity theft is a fast-growing problem in the United States. Hackers are able to tap into unprotected Internet sites and steal your identifiable information. Online shopping websites are a playground of opportunity for these scammers. Most major companies offer secure ordering, but some smaller businesses may not be equipped to offer the same security options.

Buying online is another area in which your instincts will come into play. If the ordering process does not feel right or makes you uneasy, then contact the company's customer service department by telephone or e-mail, or simply opt to move on to another website. In addition, always be sure to log out and close your browser after conducting sensitive business on the Internet. This also belays a scammer's opportunities for harvesting your information.

■ **Watch out for mock websites.** These are websites designed to resemble or imitate a well-known company or entity. Scammers will use them to gain your trust in an attempt to gather the information they want from you or to sell you a product or service.

There are several ways you can validate the authenticity of a website:

- **The URL is a dead giveaway.** If you are signing up for a freebie from a major corporation such as Pillsbury, their web address will most likely be www.pillsbury.com or a very close version to the actual company name such as www.pillsburybaking.com. A mock website will use a variation of the corporation's name in the URL but will also usually contain a longer string in the address. For example, a website that reads www.geocities/premierweb/goodoffer/pillsbury.com is probably a fraudulent site. Most legitimate companies own their company name URL, and it will always be prominent in the address. It will not be preceded by a string of other names or characters.

- **There are obvious misspellings and typing errors.** If the website contains excessive typographical or grammatical errors, it is often the sign of an amateur website set up for fraudulent activity. Professional companies hire writers and webmasters to develop their image and content. Many also have editors review the content prior to publishing their information on Internet pages. It is highly unlikely that a name brand or well-known company would allow an offer to be set up by someone with poor writing or design skills.

- **You can't find the parent company.** There will be a lack of links back to the supporting company. For example, if Pillsbury is offering a sign-up for free coupons, there will be a link from the coupon page to the main Pillsbury website. If you are unable to find a link to the home source or any links giving information about the company, promotion, and contacts, it is probably a scam.

- **It asks for unnecessary details.** Watch out for websites that require too much information or very personal information. For example, if you are signing up for a free tube of toothpaste, it would be highly unlikely that the company would need to know your mother's maiden name, your social security number, or the hospital you were born in. Mother's maiden name is commonly used as the security question to access your credit card accounts. Offering this seemingly harmless information to an unknown source could be detrimental to your financial security. Use your internal radar when it comes to doling out your private information on the Internet. Only give out information you are comfortable sharing.

- **The dates are old.** The website contains incorrect or older dates on the screen. Many scammers who set up false websites will use a "snapshot" picture of the real website. Often the real website has the date embedded in the image or has news of upcoming events posted on the website. If you visit a website in June and see that the upcoming events news posted is for events that occurred in March, challenge the content, links, and location. You have more than likely stumbled on a mock website.

■ **Beware of generic e-mail addresses.** Offers that come from individuals using free e-mail services such as Yahoo! and Hotmail are speculative at best. Quality companies have their own e-mail address and would not use a nontraceable source. JohnDoe@yahoo.com is probably not going to make you wealthy overnight, however JohnDoe@momdotcom.net may actually have something of interest to offer you.

■ **Ignore e-mails that are not addressed to you.**
E-mails that are addressed to another user virtually spell scam.
If your e-mail address is marysue@charter.net and you receive
an e-mail indicating the recipient as marymary@charter.net, it
is not a message intended for you nor is it one that accidentally showed up in your mailbox. It came from an automatic
mailing system that is targeting similar e-mail names. Don't
bother to read it—just hit the Delete button.

In addition, you may find that you receive messages with
your e-mail address listed in the recipient line along with similar addresses at the same ISP mailing account. These also
come from automated mailing systems set up to target you and
other users with similar name accounts. These automated systems randomly generate like names expecting that some will
bounce back as unknown addresses, but banking on the fact
that the majority will make it to an unsuspecting recipient
such as you. It is not only important to notice who generated
the message, but also to check who the intended recipient is.

■ **Watch out for bulk e-mails.** If a message is addressed
to multiple recipients, it is either coming from a mailing list
you signed up for or from a person/company trying to scam
you. Read each bulk mail with skepticism unless you are confident that you have requested information from the company
soliciting you.

*I t's a good thing I checked with the gals on my forum
board before I responded to that e-mail asking me to
verify my PayPal account information. They saved me a
load of headaches letting me know it was bogus.*

—STEPHANIE, *South Carolina*

■ **Avoid all requests for an up-front fee.** If they are asking you to shell out money from your pocket to get information, just say no! You should not have to pay to get a list of
survey companies, information about doing data entry work

at home, or a guide to low-cost pharmacies on the Web. These are all common scams and are to be avoided. Bottom line: do not jeopardize your hard-earned cash for the promise of wealth. The truth of the matter is that most of the information is already available if you know where to look, and if the offer is valid, the company will be willing to give you the basic information for free.

Note: Some legitimate business opportunities may require an investment fee to obtain a business kit. These are typically home business opportunities that allow the user to resell the company's products for a commission. There may be a small up-front investment to obtain display products to enhance your sales prospects. However, the company will provide you with company information, structure, and everything else you need to know in the beginning *without* charging a fee for it. They will not charge you a "membership fee" to join their program, and you will be accepted as a consultant without having to pay a dime for the privilege.

When it comes to paying for a sales kit, the questions to ask are as follows: What is in the kit? Is it worth the amount of money I'm being asked to invest? Is it a one-time fee, or will I have to pay more down the road? If the kit is of value and does not carry a further commitment to future purchases, it may be worth exploring the offer further. Always read the fine print before making an investment. In addition, it is wise to check out the company thoroughly before making a long-term commitment.

How to Research a Company

You are hooked on a website or idea that does not appear to be a scam, but you still have a lingering doubt or two. What do you do next? How do you investigate the company further to ensure that you are dealing with a reputable source? Follow these guidelines to help validate the company you are interested in:

- **Consult the Better Business Bureau (BBB) website (www.bbb.org).** The BBB will list any current information available on the organization and will give you information about its standing as a company. You will be able to see whether there have been any complaints filed and what the resolutions were. The BBB doesn't currently require Internet companies to file, but you will find that most valid, web-based firms choose to register on their own initiative. Be certain to consult the BBB's work-at-home schemes information. This listing is a current record of prominent scams on the Internet and how to recognize them.

- **Check with your state attorney general's office or the chamber of commerce.** Consult these organizations for the area in which the company's main facility is located. Contact them by phone, e-mail, or standard mail to find out more about the business you are researching. Both of these sources should be able to give you details on the company, including date of incorporation and whether it is under investigation for fraudulent activities.

- **Check with Dun & Bradstreet (www.dnb.com/us).** This listing will have a current rating for the company if it is publicly traded. You will also be given the option of purchasing more detailed information about the company.

- **Contact a customer service representative from the company you are researching.** Ask to obtain a copy of their annual report. If they do not have an annual report available for review, ask the representative to provide a list of their annual revenues, length of time in business, and contact information for at least three references who can speak of their experience with the company. Be sure to follow up and contact all of the references provided. Ask about their working relationship with the company and their level of satisfaction. Here are some sample questions you may consider asking:

- How long have you been working with Company X?
- What is the nature of your relationship with Company X?
- How would you describe Company X's level of customer service and support?
- Did they respond in a timely fashion?
- Have you encountered any hidden fees or complications?
- What is your overall impression of Company X?

■ **Get the facts.** Obtain all the information you possibly can about the company and the offer you are considering. Look for hidden costs like shipping and handling charges, monthly sales quotas, late fees, or other charges. Check for their refund policy and make certain that they have one.

■ **Read and reread the fine print.** Are you required to provide credit card information? If you sign up for the offer, will you be required to cancel within a certain time frame before your credit card is charged? Do you have to commit to purchasing additional products in order to secure the free offer? When and how will you get paid? Is there a clear statement regarding how payouts are distributed? What do you have to do to get paid? Are there sales quotas? Are there stringent requirements you need to meet? Will the company deny payment if you do not meet all the requirements? A good survey or mystery shopping company will never ask you to commit your time only to find out that your odds of getting reimbursement are nil. They may have requirements, but their expectations will be reasonable and easily fulfilled by most individuals.

■ **Ask your friends and family what they know about the company.** See whether any of the people on the boards or forums you regularly visit have any knowledge or experience with the company. People you associate with can sometimes be your best resource.

■ **Do a little private-eye work.** Research current scams
on websites such as ScamBusters (www.scambusters.org) to see
whether the company or offer you are looking at is listed. Also,
contact the National Fraud Information Center at (800) 876-
7060 for any information reported about the company.

■ **Consult the Federal Trade Commission (FTC)
"Dirty Dozen" list.** The FTC's Dirty Dozen list can be found
on its website (www.ftc.gov). The list is composed of the top
twelve e-mail scams currently circulating on the Internet.

If you come across a scam or fraudulent company, be sure
to send an e-mail with the website or e-mail information of the
scam you encountered to the FTC (uce@ftc.gov). Mail the
same information to the National Fraud Information Center,
P.O. Box 65868, Washington, DC 20035, or call (800) 876-
7060.

Following these basic guidelines will help you avoid being
scammed out of your valuable time and hard-earned dollars.
Knowledge is a powerful weapon against scam artists and other
Internet wrongdoers. The more you know, the less effective
these scams become. When scams are no longer lucrative for
the offender, chances are the scammer(s) will simply disappear.
The best Internet consumer is an informed Internet consumer.

Chapter 12

Avoiding Spam

Spam ('spam): junk, junk, junk, and more junk e-mail
Spammer ('spam r): the person or company perpetu-
  ating the junk mail

*If someone can tell me how to put an end to all the spam
cluttering up my inbox, I swear I might name my next
child after them!*

—Rose, *Indiana*

What Is Spam, and How Do I Control It?

If you have followed the steps throughout this book and are
participating in saving your family money and earning that
extra income—congratulations! You are way ahead of the game
and will continue to reap the rewards.

One pesky side effect you may be experiencing is a little
more spam buildup in your e-mail in-box. While we are fairly

certain you encountered spam in your e-mail even before you picked up this book, delving into the rich resources of the Internet may cause spam to increase. Unfortunately, spam is flooding the Internet as more and more entrepreneurs and predators sign on to the Web. In fact, spam is not unlike the junk mail you receive daily in your regular mail. The predators are no different than the snake-oil salesmen of the past. The entrepreneurs listed are simply businesses that are ignorant to the downside of spamming prospective clients or that just don't care that you are inconvenienced by their e-mail. Many of these companies or individuals want to reach as many real people as they possibly can in hopes that you will purchase their products or services.

What can be done about this irritating problem? How do you rid yourself of this petulant plague? Just as in real life, you will not completely stop unsolicited mail from arriving, but you can definitely limit the impact. The following tips can help you deter spam from piling up in your in-box.

- **Never list your complete e-mail address on a forum or board.** For example, if you are posting information to a forum and want someone to respond to your e-mail address, do not list the actual address—such asthisisme@mye-mail .com. Instead, use "thisisme AT mye-mail.com." Many spammers use automated harvesting tools to grab addresses off websites, forums, and boards. The automated tools, often called spiders or crawlers, are designed to recognize and collect e-mail addresses by the combination string of characters separated by the @ symbol.
- **Eliminate affiliate company e-mails.** Understand that when you sign up to receive e-mails from a specific company, you may also be agreeing to receive mail from that company's affiliates as well. This can make determining what is spam and what is something you agreed to receive a little difficult to decipher. When signing up with any company, always keep an eye

out for a small box that allows you to opt out of future mailings from the main company and/or its affiliates. Always check or uncheck these boxes according to your preference. You are never under any obligation to continue accepting e-mails from a company in order to take advantage of offers such as a free sample or a contest entry.

- **Set up alternate e-mail accounts.** We cannot stress this enough—make sure you set up a "dummy" e-mail account to register for free stuff, deals, and contests. If you do hit a site that sells their e-mail address database or that participates in scam or spam activity, your main e-mail account will not be flooded with unwanted correspondence. Instead, your secondary account will bear the brunt and you will be able to identify, report, and delete the messages easily. Acquiring an additional e-mail address is not a difficult prospect. You might choose to set up an account for each of the activities you are involved in. Use your best judgment. As a general rule, having separate e-mail accounts makes it easier to narrow down where the excessive spam originates. If you find spam bombarding your mystery shopper e-mail account, then chances are that one of the mystery shopping companies you work with is sharing your address with its affiliates or may have terms that include the right to sell your address to other parties. As mentioned in previous chapters, this is one of the many reasons that it is so important to research companies before agreeing to their terms of service. Information on a company's spam policies is usually found in the privacy practices section of its website.

- **Use caution when providing your e-mail address on the Web.** If the website requesting your information looks speculative, check for signs of scams and do not provide your address. If you are skeptical but still choose to sign up, use your dummy account to subscribe.

- **Filter your e-mail.** Use the built-in filtering features of your e-mail program to delete spam before it even makes it into your mailbox. You can set your Preference option to filter messages containing words or phrases such as "Triple X" or "Viagra" to prevent pornographic or other unwanted messages from filling your in-box. If you have any questions about accessing or setting up your filtering features, contact your service provider for support. They will be able to assist you, answer your questions, and help you rid your in-box of unwanted pests.

If you decide to use the junk/bulk mail filtering that many e-mail providers offer, be sure to check your bulk mail folder on a regular basis prior to deleting the messages contained there. Occasionally a legitimate e-mail that you would want to address or read may wind up in the bulk mail folder. While spam filters do an excellent job, they are by no means perfect and can sometimes send a personal or important company e-mail to the wrong folder. In addition, you will want to check the options of the junk/bulk mail function within your e-mail program. Many of these filters have a self-deleting option in which all the bulk mail will be deleted on exiting the program or within a set time frame, such as being scheduled to delete bulk mail every three days. You may want to change these options to allow yourself adequate time to check the bulk folders for mail you would like to read or keep.

■ **Stop before you opt.** If you receive a spam e-mail with a link that lets you opt out of receiving future mailings or offers—*stop*! Do not click on the link thinking it will remove you from their mailing list. While many reputable companies will comply with your opt-out request, more often clicking on the removal link actually lets the spammers know that your e-mail address is active and maintained by a living, breathing human being. This in turn will then increase the influx of spam to your mailbox.

■ **Never respond to a spam e-mail.** Don't ever reply to a spam message asking the sender to remove you from their mailing list or even to blast them with your outrage that they are spamming you in the first place. This will have the same effect as clicking on the removal link within the message. It will confirm that you have a live address and in turn, you will receive even more spam.

The government is also working to control fraud and spam on the Internet. Congress passed a bill titled the U.S. Can Spam Act. Enacted on January 1, 2004, it prohibits the senders of unsolicited e-mail from disguising their identity. This law is the start of a movement to diminish the amount of spam on the Internet and to hold spammers accountable for their actions. More information and the complete contents of the bill can be found on the Federal Trade Commission site (www.ftc .gov) or the Spam Laws site (www.spamlaws.com).

Alternate Forms of Spam

It's my computer, it's my privacy, I'm not going to give in to some idiot who wants to compromise that.

—STEPHANIE, *Maine*

In general, spam occurs more heavily through e-mail traffic, but you will also encounter a few other types of spam while surfing the Web—in particular, pop-ups and spyware. Both are generally unwelcome annoyances, however both are easy to curb. Let's take a closer look at these two pests.

Pop-Ups

One of the more intrusive advertising methods implemented by online marketers is pop-up ads. These ads allow the advertiser to reach a large market with little effort. They always seem to appear on your computer screen at the most inopportune moments. Even worse, they are often tricky to get rid of. Once you close one pop-up window, another one seems to open instantaneously until you finally outmaneuver or close all of them.

The good news is that you are not doomed to suffer with the inconvenience of Internet pop-ups. With advances in software, pop-up blockers have come into their own and are more effective then ever. Blocker software programs are quick to install and easy to use, offer a variety of options, and can generally be customized.

There are a variety of free software pop-up blockers available, such as the Google Toolbar found on the Google website (www.googletoolbar.com). Simply run an Internet search for "free pop-up blockers" and you will be provided with several software options to choose from. There are also pop-up blocking software options included in some ISP programs, such as AOL, and retail software programs such as Norton Utilities. Whichever route you decide to go, once you implement a pop-up blocker software tool, the nuisance will be virtually eliminated from your Internet experience.

If by chance you find that you want to view a particular pop-up ad, perhaps for a free sample offer or a points program, most blocking tools provide an option for you to choose to view or not view pop-ups on an individual basis. Be sure to check the software you choose to see what convenient options are included.

Spyware

Spyware is a little tricky to define, but basically it's a software program designed to secretly track computer user activities. Spyware is not only a form of spam, it can also be considered an illegal activity in some situations. Some spyware programs are designed to deceptively harvest consumer data, lift passwords, or even copy credit card and social security numbers as well as private bank information. The United States government takes illegal spyware activities very seriously and is currently working to promote and enact laws governing the use of spyware.

The bulk of spyware programs you will encounter are designed to track your interests and Internet activities, which allows an Internet marketer to gear its advertising specifically toward you and your family. For example, if you visit a lot of websites related to pets and pet stores and find you are seeing more spam or pop-up ads for dog food, it is likely that a spyware program is installed on your computer.

So how did you get it? How did someone install such a program on your computer? More than likely, it came attached to something you downloaded off of a website or an e-mail. It may have been attached to an Internet game, a screensaver, a desktop theme, or similar freeware. You may never pinpoint exactly where the program originated. Unfortunately, the unscrupulous behavior of others becomes our burden to bear.

Should you just give up and shut down your computer? Not at all. There is an easy way to deal with spyware. This is another area where software advances come to the rescue. Thanks to programs like Ad-Aware from Lavasoft (www.lava softusa.com), it is fast and easy to find and remove spyware from your PC. If you run a search for "free spyware removal," you'll come up with various other options as well. In addition, many of the retail antivirus software programs such as Norton and McAfee contain features that rid your computer of spyware. You need only read the directions and follow the steps to delete unwanted programs, thereby keeping you and your information safe.

Do not give in to the fear of encountering spyware spam on the Internet. With a little know-how and the proper tools, you will easily outsmart the people attempting to invade your privacy.

More Helpful Advice Regarding Spam

Never, ever, under any circumstances send anyone your password or registration information for any website or e-mail account. If you receive an e-mail requesting private information, such as your password to your eBay or bank account or your credit card or social security number—do not respond! A reputable company will never ask you to provide sensitive information via e-mail. If you do happen to receive a spam e-mail requesting private information, be sure to report it immediately to the Federal Trade Commission or the National Fraud Information Center, as well as the company mentioned in the fraudulent message.

Spam can also take the form of false information. Generally these types of spam are initiated by someone who is playing a prank or by someone who is trying to impose a biased point of view on a topic or situation. Examples include the following:

- You receive an e-mail about a lost child that asks you to forward it to everyone you know in hopes of finding him or her. While this could actually be a legitimate request, the sad fact is most of them are not.
- You receive a message telling you that if you forward it to ten friends, Microsoft will send you a check for $250 because they are running a test to track their e-mail software. Don't you wish it were that easy to make money? Unfortunately, it is one whopper of a scam.
- You receive an e-mail alerting you that a friend has inadvertently sent a virus to your computer. The message gives you instructions to rid your computer of the virus, usually by suggesting that you delete a file off your hard drive. Stop! Do not follow those instructions. Chances are you have just been spammed. If you need information on removing a virus from your computer, you should always look to your antivirus soft-

ware provider or computer manufacturer first. These companies house the most up-to-date and reliable information.
Always verify the information before deleting any files from
your PC. Often it is a file that your computer requires to run
properly. A good resource to check if you have questions about
the validity of an e-mail message is the Snopes website (www
.snopes.com). Snopes holds a comprehensive database of current and past spam e-mails. You will be able to find out the
truth and the lies about the particular "urban legend" you've
received.

Viruses and E-Mail Worms

These are the most malicious forms of spam. With antivirus
programs being used in conjunction with ISP software on
home computers today, the threat has lessened but is still
worth mentioning. There are steps you can take to ensure that
you are not the victim of a virus through your e-mail.

■ **Install an antivirus program on your home computer and have it set to scan your incoming e-mail.** There
are lots of programs to choose from, and many will achieve the
desired effect. One important feature that you should look for
is the ability to update on a regular basis so that you stay current and protected against new viruses and threats. Antivirus
software typically comes with an auto update feature that
updates information on current viruses independently while
you are logged on to the Internet.

■ **Do not open any e-mail attachments unless you
trust the person who sent them.** If you do not recognize the
sender or the message appears to be spam, delete it without
opening any attached files. Even if you are using a virus protection program to scan your files, it's still better to be safe than
sorry. Some of the common file extensions that carry viruses
are .exe, .com, .scr, .pif, and .bat. You may even receive a virus

from known, trusted sources without those sources realizing it was sent from their computer. If you receive an e-mail from your mother with an attachment that looks suspicious, your safest bet is to verify that she actually sent the message prior to opening it and downloading the file. Another tip for spotting potential virus-carrying e-mails: many of these virus writers will name their file attachments with common names that are familiar to you, such as virtualflowers.exe or acardforyou .exe, thereby taking advantage of your trust to launch an attack on your computer.

If you really feel the need to download the attachment, regardless of its suspicious nature, make sure to save the file and scan it using your virus software prior to opening it.

When all else fails, there is the handy Delete button. Spam, short of viruses, is really nothing more than an annoyance. While we can all live without it, chances are spam will remain a distasteful side effect of the Internet experience. The key is to use the tips and information available to you to limit its occurrence so you can enjoy your time online.

Part 2

Putting Your Saving Savvy to Work

Chapter 13
Baby

*W*hen I found out I was pregnant, I never thought in a million years that I would be able to afford all the baby essentials. Thanks to the Internet, not only can I afford the things I need, but the things I want, too.

—MARIA, *San Diego*

One of the biggest financial impacts experienced by a mother is the introduction of a new baby to the family budget. Whether you are a first-time parent or a mother of five, your newest addition will be accompanied by an ever-increasing need for expensive extras.

Don't despair; simply using the basics of our methodology will save you a mint. To further maximize savings, we've included some baby extras and Internet hotspots to ensure that your new addition does not deter you from your shopping-savvy mission.

This chapter offers a quick hit for popular baby items such as diapers, formula, and furniture. Remember, these tips and guidelines are to be used in conjunction with the methods you've already learned.

Formula

If you chose to formula feed or even formula supplement, the costs can add up quickly while you keep your baby happy and well fed. On average, it may cost anywhere from $4 to $12 or more a day to keep your little one supplied with healthy nutrients. An excellent way to reduce your expenses is to enroll in the baby programs established by the formula companies. These programs typically give you access to product samples and coupons that will help curb your costs. Here are some baby formula websites to get you started on your path to savings:

- Enfamil (www.enfamil.com)
- Nestle (www.verybestbaby.com)
- Similac (www.similac.com)
- Nature's One (www.naturesone.com)
- Bright Beginnings (www.brightbeginnings.com)
- Parent's Choice (www.parentschoiceformula.com)

In addition to enrolling with the manufacturer programs, consider following these suggestions:

■ **Ask your pediatrician for samples and coupons.** Formula companies know that formula selection begins at the hospital and with doctor recommendations. Typically, these companies will leave samples and coupons with medical offices for the doctor to distribute. At each visit, simply ask your health care provider for any samples or coupons he or she might have. Physicians and nurses are generally very willing to help, and the savings will truly add up over time.

■ **Swap coupons with other moms of newborns.** Check with your friends, family, and Internet forum buddies to see who might have a need for the coupons you don't want and vice versa. It's a great way to help each other manage the formula budget.

- **Check to see whether your state offers a Women, Infants, Children (WIC) program and find out if you qualify.** You may be able to receive assistance with your formula needs. For more information, visit the United States Department of Agriculture Food and Nutrition website (www.fns .usda.gov/wic).
- **Watch for periodic sales on formula at your favorite grocers and retailers.** Use these sales in combination with your coupons to stock up and obtain maximum savings.

Diapers

Whether you chose cloth or conventional diapers, the cost will add up over the first two to three years of your child's life. Here are a few websites where you'll gain access to tips, coupons, and special offers:

- Huggies (www.huggies.com)
- Pampers (www.pampers.com)
- Goodnites (www.goodnites.com)
- Stork's Choice (www.storkschoice.com)

Along with diapers, you'll need toiletries to help keep baby dry, fresh, and clean. There are many websites where you'll be sure to find a wealth of samples and coupons for diaper creams, bathing products, and baby-related items. Here are a few sites to get you started:

- Gerber (www.gerber.com)
- babyADE (www.babyade.com)
- Orajel (www.orajel.com)
- Desitin (www.desitin.com)
- Johnson & Johnson (www.johnsonsbaby.com)
- Playtex Baby (www.playtexbaby.com)

When thinking about baby care items, keep the following in mind:

■ Sample products come in handy sizes that are perfect for packing in the diaper bag. Along with enrolling in baby programs and signing up for free samples on the Internet, also keep an eye out at your local grocer, baby superstores, and doctor's office for sample offerings.

■ If you choose to use cloth diapers, their resale value on auction sites or through private sales generally stays consistent. Check with these online locations before purchasing your diapers; you may snag some great deals, as well as be able to sell your unused or "like new" diapers when your baby outgrows the need for them.

■ If you choose to use conventional diapers, be sure to use your coupon skills to maximize your savings. Watch for sales and use your coupons to stock up during peak sales activity. Also, consider trying a variety of diapers until you settle on what type and brand suit your child best. This will allow you to take advantage of multiple sales and coupon opportunities, and you may find that a generic brand works well for you and saves your budget from extra strain.

Layettes, Equipment, and Furniture

Sleepers, blankets, strollers, cribs, playpens, high chairs, car seats, and walkers—the list seems endless when preparing for your baby's safety, comfort, and convenience. These items need not break the bank if you use the lessons you've learned with us. After you determine which items you need, keep these rules in mind:

• Safety first.
• Shop around.

Check out auction websites and your favorite forums for deals. Consider swapping for some of the items you need. Whatever you do, be sure to take the time to find the best bang for your buck. Some websites that may help in your quest are the following:

- Discount Baby Furniture (www.discount-baby furniture.net)
- Baby Loot Classifieds (www.babyloot.com)
- Kiddicare (www.kiddicare.com)
- BizRate Shopping Search (www.bizrate.com)

Throughout your search for suitable clothing and baby items, always keep your infant's safety in mind. Be careful to choose high-quality products that meet current safety standards. A good resource for keeping up on the latest product developments and safety standards is the United States Consumer Product Safety Commission website (www.cpsc.com). Here are some other useful websites:

- National Safe Kids Campaign (www.safekids.org)
- American Academy of Pediatrics (www.aap.org)
- Recalls.gov (www.recalls.gov)

They'll provide a wealth of information on baby-related products, pricing, features, and the best ways to keep baby safe.

Food, Snacks, and Other Items

Your little one won't last on formula alone for very long. Baby-specific foods will soon become a routine item on your shopping list. You'll have an easy time using your coupon savvy and bargain hunting skills to keep your cupboard well stocked, but here are a few extra tips that might help.

■ Be sure to sign up for baby food company programs. Here are a few to get you started:

- Gerber (www.gerber.com)
- Heinz (www.heinzbaby.com)
- Earth's Best (www.earthsbest.com)
- Beech-Nut (www.beechnut.com)

■ Consider making your own baby foods. Here are two websites with information to get you moving in the right direction:

- Healthy Baby Food (www.healthy-baby-food.com)
- Wholesome Baby Food (www.wholesomebaby food.com)

■ Also check with the National Network for Child Care (NNCC) website (www.nncc.org) and the United States Food and Drug Administration (FDA) Center for Food Safety and Applied Nutrition website (www. cfsan.fda.gov) for the latest information on food safety before trying any recipes on your own.

■ As we mentioned earlier in the formula section of this chapter, check to see if your state offers a Women, Infants, Children program. WIC also offers a nutrition and food program for older children.

A Few More Quick Tips

Here are some extras to help you economize during the baby years.

■ **Enroll for free baby magazine subscriptions.** Inside each issue you will find great tips, articles, and often money-saving coupons. Here are a few that may offer free trials:

- American Baby (www.americanbaby.com)
- Baby Talk (www.parenting.com/parenting)
- Parents (www.parents.com)

■ **Update your survey profiles.** Having a newborn is definitely a plus to your survey profile. Babies are a focus for many companies that are dying to know your opinions and suggestions for their product lines. Be sure to update your profile with each survey company you are enrolled with as soon as you know the expected birth date of your child. It is important to input this information during your pregnancy; you may find it opens up opportunities for you to participate in prenatal studies or sample maternity-related products.

■ **Notify your mystery shopping companies to change your profile.** Think that your newborn will not have an impact on your mystery shopping assignments? Reconsider that thought—many companies will open up new assignments for you based on your family makeup. Ideally, who better to visit a maternity clothing store than an expectant mom? If you are a new mom, you may also want to find out if there are any companies seeking new mothers for participation in their programs.

■ **Having twins?** If you are expecting twins, your wallet will take twice the hit it would with a single child. E-mail or write to the major manufacturers of your favorite baby products to see whether they offer special discounts or free merchandise to parents of twins (or triplets, or more).

■ **Consider the "after" value.** As you are making purchases, keep in mind their resale value, especially when it comes to short-term items like infant carriers and newborn clothing. It may sway your purchase decision knowing what you will be able to resell these items for in an online auction or through private transactions. Think about swapping and trading for some of the baby items you need. You don't have to swap baby items for baby items. Think about what other products you have to offer and trade away to savings.

■ **Purchase from other moms.** Look on auction, trading, and swapping sites for the items you need. You may find a fabulous bargain from another mom.

Parenting Resources

Parenting resources are abundant on the Net. Whether you need advice regarding potty training, eating habits, or just feeling overwhelmed as a mother, the information you seek can be found on the Net.

Here are a few websites that include resources for expectant moms, new parents, and seasoned pros:

- American Baby (www.americanbaby.com)
- Parent Soup (www.parentsoup.com)
- Parent Stages (www.parentstages.com)

Remember to network with others. You'll be sure to find all the baby tips and advice you need!

Chapter 14

Toddler to Teen

*M*y teens can break the bank without even trying. Thank goodness I am a shopping-savvy mom or we'd be in the poorhouse.

—ALICE, *New Mexico*

Before you know it, those goo-goo-eyed babies grow into walking, talking toddlers, and then don't-you-wish-they-were-babies-again teens. These growth spurts bring with them a whole new set of challenges.

No need to throw in the towel. As with babies, all the basics of our methodology will apply. This chapter offers a quick hit for toddler to teen topics such as fashion, activities, and school. We've included our best tips for keeping your budget in check and your sanity intact.

Food and Fashion

Sometimes our children grow so fast it seems they consume half the household groceries with each breath they take or change clothing sizes overnight. Along with the money-saving skills you learned in Part 1, here are some extra tips and resources to help you keep up with your sprouting and hungry crew.

■ **Start or join a clothing exchange with other moms.** Gather together your friends, neighbors, or online pals with children and begin a clothing exchange circle. The idea is to swap, trade, hand down, or sell clothing to each other as your children grow in and out of them. Be sure to establish a set of guidelines or a loose structure for the group, and you'll all benefit from the exchange.

■ **Get creative with snacks and meals.** Keep your kids eating healthier and interested in all the food groups by having a variety of options on hand. Here are a few websites to help you out with ideas:

- All Recipes After School Energy Boosters (www .allrecipes.com/features/backtoschool.asp)
- Just Kids Recipes (www.justkidsrecipes.com)
- Kids Health (www.kidshealth.org)
- National Network for Child Care (www.nncc.org)

Parties

What could be more fun than celebrating your baby's first birthday? Why, celebrating all the birthdays that follow. Whether you have a casual family gathering or a full-blown bash, here are some websites and ideas to ensure an enjoyable time for all:

- Birthday Party Ideas (www.birthdaypartyideas.com)
- Kids Parties Connection (www.kidsparties.com)
- BHG Birthday Party Games (www.bhg.com/home/Birth day-Party-Games.html)

Also, consider sending electronic invitations to invite your guests; you'll save on paper and postage. Popular greeting card websites such as Hallmark (www.hallmark.com) and American Greetings (www.americangreetings.com) have multiple options to choose from.

Activities

Once your children get past the age of rattles, it becomes increasingly challenging to keep them entertained. In addition, you may be concerned about their level of physical activity and the quality of their sedentary activities. Here are some websites and suggestions to help you keep your children busy with brain-stimulating, hands-on, heart-healthy activities.

Active Minds

It may take a village to raise a child, but it only takes a short trip to the Internet to find age-appropriate learning games and activities to keep their synapses buzzing. The next time you are looking for rainy day activities or help with particular learning areas, try these websites:

- Yahooligans (www.yahooligans.yahoo.com)
- Learning Disabilities Online (www.ldonline.com)
- Enchanted Learning (www.enchantedlearning.com/home.html)
- Council for Exceptional Children (www.cec.sped.org)
- Fun Brain (www.funbrain.com)
- Family Education Network (www.familyeducation.com)
- Scholastic (www.scholastic.com)

Creative Hands

Do you ever find yourself at a loss for things to do on those days when the kids are restless or bored? Here are a few websites to help you out with crafts and creative ideas galore:

- Disney's FamilyFun (www.familyfun.go.com)
- Free Kid Crafts (www.freekidcrafts.com)
- Idea Box (www.theideabox.com)
- Handcrafter's Village (www.handcraftersvillage.com)
- Canon Print Planet (www.canonprintplanet.com/kids)

Don't forget to use your bargain shopping skills to save on craft supplies.

Bodies in Motion

Do you want to encourage your child to have a love of sports, the great outdoors, or other exercise options? Look to the Internet as a resource, and check out the following websites:

- The National Bone Health Campaign (www.cdc.gov/powerfulbones/index_content.html)
- 4 Girls Health (www.4girls.gov)
- Girl Power! (www.girlpower.gov)
- Ready Set Go (www.readysetgo.org)
- Fitness.gov (www.fitness.gov)
- Active.com (www.active.com)
- Be Active Kids (www.beactivekids.org)
- KidsGardening (www.kidsgardening.com)

If you need outdoor supplies or sports gear, you already have the shopping savvy skills to save a bundle. So what are you waiting for? Get moving with your children and have some fun.

School

Going to school encompasses a large part of the toddler through teenage years. Coursework has changed and supplies have changed, too. Whether your child attends public, private, or home school, use these Internet links to find the information and supplies you need:

- Macmillan McGraw-Hill (www.mhschool.com)
- Homeschool World (www.home-school.com)
- Great Schools (www.greatschools.net)
- Discovery School (www.school.discovery.com)

Another aspect of school to consider is homework. With our rapidly changing knowledge of the universe, it's difficult for us to keep up with every aspect of our child's education. Finding the right resource to help with questions you may not be able to answer can be invaluable to you and your children. Here are a few websites to get you started:

- Infoplease Homework Center (www.infoplease.com/homework)
- The Open Door Web Site (www.knockonthedoor.com)
- Schoolwork Ugh! (www.schoolwork.org)
- High School Hub (www.highschoolhub.org)

Continuing and advanced education options for your child may be an area you want to begin exploring even before they enter preschool. To help you get started with ideas for saving for college or ways to equip your children with life skills, we listed a few websites that you may want to view:

- Study Guides and Strategies (www.studygs.net)
- U.S. Department of Education (www.ed.gov)
- UPromise (www.upromise.com)

Chapter 15
Mom and Dad

*M*y husband says I am a shopaholic, but even he couldn't complain once he realized how much money we were actually saving!

—SUSAN, *Delaware*

Parents need extras, too, but of course when it comes to sacrificing, Mom and Dad are generally the ones to do so. Sometimes you are simply looking for a new recipe, and other times you desire that "something special" just for you. The tips presented in this chapter, used in conjunction with the techniques we've already discussed, will allow you the opportunity to say yes to the special little extras more often.

Time Savers

Time is the one luxury you don't want to skimp on. Tips to save time, energy, and money around the house are always welcome. There are several websites out there that offer tricks of trade via a web page and/or newsletters. Cleaning, cooking, shopping, organizing—information for all of these is readily available on the Internet. Stay up-to-date on your favorite company's products, or check for coupons. Here are a few websites to save you time and get you started:

- P&G brandSaver (www.brandsaver.com)
- All Your Rooms (www.allyourrooms.com)
- Organized Home (www.organizedhome.com)
- Women Central (www.womencentral.net)
- FlyLady (www.flylady.net)
- Home Made Simple (www.homemadesimple.com)

Pick and choose the methods and ideas that work best for you. Remember that the key is to simplify your life to allow time for luxuries.

Frugal Folks

When we think of luxury, we often think of big-ticket items. Have you ever really wanted something for yourself, but you were a few dollars short? Check out these frugal family sites for even more ways to stretch your dollars. You will find tips, tricks, free printables, and even recipes to make your own homemade laundry detergent. You'll also find information on how to add luxuries to your life without the high price tag attached. You never know what you will find, so be sure to look around, there is a lot to learn. Here are a few sites with information and ideas:

- Frugal Mom (www.frugalmom.net)
- Miserly Moms (www.miserlymoms.com)
- The Frugal Shopper (www.thefrugalshopper.com)
- Frugal Families (www.frugal-families.com)
- DIY Network (www.diynet.com)

Hobbies

Resources for hobbies ranging from crafts to fitness can be found everywhere on the Web. Get your gear or supplies cheaper by using coupon codes, check for free issues or subscriptions of your favorite hobby-related magazines, and always be on the lookout for people who have the same hobbies or interests as you.

Whatever your leisure interest is, you may want to capture the memories on film—after all, your main "hobby" is probably your family and children. Whether your interest is digital or standard photography, you may want to print your pictures to share with friends and relatives or for scrapbooking. Here are a few tips to guide you along the way:

■ You have the technology at hand, why not use it? Consider creating, managing, and fixing the flaws in your photographs on your own computer and printing them yourself if you own a photo-capable printer. Multiple websites offer tips, guidelines on how to get started, cost comparisons, and even free software. Here are a few to look at:

- Kodak (www.kodak.com)
- Hewlett Packard (www.hp.com)
- Creative Paper Crafts (www.yourcreativespirit .com)
- Hanes T-ShirtMaker (www.hanes2u.com/soft ware/deluxe/deluxe.htm)

■ If you do not have a high-quality photo printer, or if your printer guzzles ink when printing in color, you may want to consider using a "traditional" developer or online photo developer for your printing needs. Check out your local retailers to see what they charge for high-quality digital prints, or consider using online developers such as these:

- Snapfish (www.snapfish.com)
- Kodak Easy Share Gallery (www.kodakgallery .com)
- Shutterfly (www.shutterfly.com)

■ Does your photo passion include scrapbooking? Check out Frugal Scrap Booking (www.frugalscrapbooking.com) for tips and tricks to scrap on a shoestring budget, and the Scrapbook Scrapbook (www.scrapbookscrapbook.com) for printables, templates, and tips.

There are so many hobbies, we'd be hard-pressed to cover them all, but here are a few craft and hobby sites that may offer freebies and information to capture your interest:

- Crayola (www.crayola.com)
- Disney's FamilyFun (www.familyfun.go.com)
- About Hobbies and Games (www.about.com/hobbies)
- Fitness Online (www.fitnessonline.com)
- Just Move (www.justmove.org)
- Aunt Annie's Crafts (www.auntannie.com)

Cooking is a popular hobby that fits in well with the principles we've introduced in this book by offering frugal options, luxury, and numerous ways to use your shopping-savvy skills. Regardless of who does the cooking in your house, we bet the chef du jour frequently finds himself or herself wanting to try something new. There are thousands of free recipes available via the Internet. Wondering where to find recipes? Some good places to start are as follows:

- All Recipes (www.allrecipes.com)
- Food Network (www.foodtv.com)
- Top Secret Recipes (www.topsecretrecipes.com)
- Epicurious (www.epicurious.com)

In addition, you'll find many newsletters to subscribe to. Many of these publications will include recipes and even money-saving coupons. Here are a few that you may want to consider:

- Kraft Kitchens (www.kraftfoods.com)
- Hershey's Kitchens (www.hersheys.com)
- Hunt's Club (www.hunts.com)
- Chef Mom (www.chefmom.com)
- FamilyFun Recipes Newsletter (www.register.go.com/family/recipes/login)
- Crisco Cooks (www.crisco.com/subscribe.asp)
- Red & Yellow's Bright Ideas (www.marsbrightideas.com)

While you are signing up for the newsletters, don't forget to look around these websites for a wealth of other information as well.

Also, ask your Internet peers what their families' favorite recipes are or visit food-friendly forums. Recipe swapping is a surefire way to liven up your kitchen creations.

Additional Tips for Hobby Enthusiasts

Here is an extra hodge-podge of ideas to help you make the most of your hobbies.

■ **Give gifts from the heart.** Consider giving homemade gifts for birthdays, holidays, or other momentous occasions. If you have a friend who collects candles and you recently took up candle making as a hobby, why not show off your skills and make your friend a beautiful and thoughtful gift basket? Know someone who likes to bake but hardly has the time? Give them cookie or brownie mix in a jar, with a handwritten recipe attached for that added personal touch. There are also some creative websites offering ideas for gifts with a homemade touch, such as the All Free Crafts website (www.allfreecrafts .com) and the Crafty-Moms website (www.crafty-moms.com).

In addition, consider selling your homemade crafts to others on auction sites or other websites such as Ehomecrafts (www.ehomecrafts.com).

■ **Consider teaming up.** Ordering in bulk often saves you a lot of money. If you know four or five other moms who have interests similar to yours, you might consider ordering craft kits or items in bulk, then splitting the costs equally among the participants with a small amount added for shipping and handling.

■ **Use your search skills.** Whatever your interests may be, smart searching will yield a wide variety of results to choose from. Determine the best keywords needed to produce the most productive results, and you are sure to find what you're looking for.

■ **Ask your online communities for help.** Are you not sure which site is best for craft supplies? Want to find out whether there are any free fitness magazines available? As you already know, your online community can be your biggest ally in your search for information. Check with members for their experiences, thoughts, or ideas on the best homemade gifts to give, cheapest magazine subscriptions, most affordable online shopping sites, and favorite websites geared toward your interests.

The focus on mom and dad doesn't end here. See Chapters 17 and 18 for tips on vacationing and entertainment to add more luxuries and pampering to your life!

Chapter 16

Household

Y*ou could have knocked me over with a feather when I got my electric bill this month. Who would have thought using the Internet could actually save me money on electricity?*

—JEAN, *Alabama*

No matter how you slice it, running a household can be an expensive proposition. The Internet is loaded with information designed to help you become more efficient at it.

Big-Ticket Items

You'd really like a new coffee table, but your husband wants a new stereo receiver, and the kids have been begging you for a portable DVD player. Your budget will only allow for two of these items. Will you have to give up your dream of a new coffee table to accommodate your family's wishes? Not necessarily. All three things can be purchased without breaking the bank by a savvy shopper.

You will be able to use the same bargain hunting skills you learned in Chapter 2 for expensive items from furniture to major household appliances. There are a few extra tricks you'll want to be privy to, though. In this chapter, we've detailed the tips you'll need to stretch your dollars and accommodate all of your family's desires—including your own.

- **Consider shipping options.** Shipping can be costly on larger or more expensive items. Some sellers are not even willing to ship these items and allow local pickup only. To find the best value, you may choose to shop online and then purchase at a retail store, especially if you have the means to transport the item yourself. Either way, always ask about shipping options and costs prior to committing to a purchase.
- **Take your time.** The coffee table you want may be full price now, but in just a week or two, it may be 25 percent off or more. Be patient when buying expensive items, strike when the iron is hot and never pay full price.
- **Consider buying last year's model.** Buying a discontinued model may save you a bundle of cash.
- **Dents and scratches.** Items are often marked down substantially when they have a scratch or dent. Most scratches are easily touched up, and if the dented side of the refrigerator will go against a wall, why not save some money? The only one who will know about the imperfections is you.
- **Check online auctions.** When making a large purchase such as furnishings, you may wish to limit your search to local auctioneers only. You can e-mail them and ask if it is possible for you to take a look at the piece before you bid, ensuring that the condition, color, and other important details are right for you.
- **Ask your online peers.** Perhaps someone in your online community has something similar to what you're looking for, and they want to get it out of their basement or garage. There's no harm in asking, because you never know what you

may find. Always be sure to use caution when meeting Internet comrades for the first time. You may want to bring friends with you or meet in a neutral location, such as a store parking lot or a restaurant. Unfortunately, you can never be too careful, and no matter what you do online, you must always consider your own safety first. In addition, check out the American Bar Association's Safe Shopping website (www.safeshopping .org) for additional tips and recommended safety practices for Internet purchases. When you are committing a large amount of cash to a purchase, it's prudent to be a smart and safe shopper.

■ **Look to the Internet for the best tricks of the trade.** Many websites offer a wealth of information on big-ticket items, as well as ways for you to save. Here are a few to get you started:

- Furniture Shopping Tips (www.furniture shoppingtips.com)
- FurnitureFan (www.furniturefan.com)
- MySimon (www.mysimon.com). Offers top product lists; comparison shopping; and tips for electronics, computers, jewelry, and more.
- Major Appliance Shopping Guide (www.eere .energy.gov/consumerinfo/energy_savers/ shoppingguide.html)
- CNET (www.cnet.com). News, reviews, and guides for technology products such as computers and consumer electronics
- Jewelry Information Center (www.jic.org)

Utilities

Most of the civilized world could not live without the modern conveniences of electricity and running water. We all sit on our computers and surf the Net in a warm, comfortable house and simply pay the monthly bills as a matter of course.

The Internet can help save you money on your utility bills. Well, not directly, but there are tons of websites that offer tips and tricks to help lower your electric, heating, and water bills, saving you money on the things you can't live without. Check with your local gas and electric companies to see what you can do to conserve energy as well as how to make the most efficient use of your energy. Also, see if your supplier offers a budget plan as a payment option. When you choose the budget plan, you will pay the same amount for your utilities monthly, regardless of usage. This helps a lot of people, as a varying bill can make it more difficult to plan your monthly finances.

Here are some websites that offer sound advice for lowering the costs of your utilities:

- U.S. Department of Energy (www.energy.gov)
- Alliance to Save Energy (www.ase.org)
- American Water Works Association (www.awwa.org)

In addition there are numerous frugality-oriented and business websites with utility-saving information and articles to give you ideas and tips for saving. A few we found to get you started are the following:

- PowerHouse (www.powerhousetv.com)
- Energyshop (www.energyshop.com)
- Home Energy Online (www.homeenergy.org/hewebsite/consumerinfo/index.html)
- Thames Water Wise Website (www.thameswateruk.co.uk/waterwise)
- Frugal World (www.frugalworld.com/utilities_tips.htm)

Don't forget to ask around for more energy-saving tips. See what friends and family are doing to save energy and water. Ask your online communities, too; you'll be surprised at the things you've never thought of. For example, lowering your thermostat one degree in the winter can save up to 3 percent on your heating bill.

Automobiles

The Internet is brimming with information about both used and new vehicles. You can read about people's individual experiences, research vehicles, compare pricing, and even scope out dealership specifics prior to walking onto a car lot. Vehicle purchases are investments, and it's always best to shop around. Here are some hard-hitting tips to help you along the way to finding the perfect vehicle.

- **Determine the type(s) of vehicle you are interested in purchasing.** Begin by researching vehicles directly on the manufacturers' websites. While you are there, look for manufacturer incentives such as cash back, special finance rates, or incentives to test-drive a vehicle. Make a note of the offers that appeal to you.

  If you are searching for older or used vehicles, consider browsing websites such as Edmunds (www.edmunds.com), Cars.com (www.cars.com), or CarMax (www.carmax.com) to find makes and models of interest to you. Note the availability and pricing.
- **Dig deeper for more information.** Websites such as Edmunds (www.edmunds.com) offer vehicle specs, manufacturer incentives, and reviews. You may also find individual auto reviews on the Epinions website (www.epinions.com).

  If those sites do not offer enough information, a simple search on your favorite search engine, using the keywords "year/make/model reviews," will land you plenty of results to peruse at your leisure.

- **Compare pricing and features.** Visit Kelley Blue Book (www.kbb.com) or NADA Guides (www.nadaguides.com) to look up prices for new vehicles and the values of used cars.
- **Keep an eye out for alternate incentives to help with your purchase.** Companies like General Motors (GM) offer reward-based credit cards with cash incentives toward new automotive purchases. Visit (www.gmcard.com) for specific information on the GM program, and check with your credit card companies to find out what incentives may be available to you to aid in your automotive purchases.

Contact your bank or credit union to find out about special finance offers or promotions. Also, find out if your employer sponsors any cooperative programs with automotive manufacturers or dealerships. You may find you are privy to additional discounts, upgrades, or services. Remember to explore every avenue.

- **Never settle for sticker price.** All prices, especially those on new vehicles, are negotiable. While the markup is not as high as you might think, there is still some wiggle room. Many auto dealerships make their money selling the extras. If your salesman tries to sell you rustproofing and undercoating, be sure to inquire whether or not that is standard on the vehicle and investigate the benefits before spending your hard-earned money on options.

The prices on used cars may not be quite as negotiable, but if the car of your dreams is for sale for $5,000 and you show up with $4,700 cash, you may find the seller is slightly more flexible then he or she may have appeared initially. More often then not, it's worth the time and effort to negotiate a fair price.

- **Browse online auctions.** Companies like eBay (www .ebay.com) have special divisions dedicated to motor vehicles. You may wish to look around for a local seller that will allow you to look at the vehicle before bidding. If you are lucky enough to find a place that has what you are looking for, be sure to take along someone who is mechanically knowledgeable or even your regular auto technician if possible. Once you have driven the car away, you will have little recourse if you've bought a lemon. As the saying goes, "caveat emptor."

Above all, have fun, take your time, and don't settle. Soon you'll be driving down the road with change to spare.

Household Projects

When it comes to home projects, you will be amazed at the extent of material available on the Internet. Information on everything from gardening to interior painting may be accessed with a click of the mouse. Here are some sites you may want to visit for pricing, tips, and how-tos when planning your next household project:

- Hometime (www.hometime.com)
- BobVila.com (www.bobvila.com)
- Don Vandervort's hometips.com (www.hometips.com)
- Home & Garden Television (www.hgtv.com)
- MSN House & Home (www.houseandhome.msn.com)

In addition, Do It Yourself (www.doityourself.com) offers tons of information and forums for you to connect with other do-it-yourselfers.

Are you more interested in decorating? Then you may find the following websites helpful:

- Better Homes and Gardens (www.bhg.com)
- Decorator Secrets (www.decoratorsecrets.com)
- Home Decorating Directory (www.allhomedecor.com)
- The Learning Channel (www.tlc.discovery.com). Home to the "Trading Spaces" TV show website and others

References

Often overlooked is the availability of free literature on the Internet. Information on topics such as home safety, finance, and health abound. Here are a few sites you might want to visit to obtain some more information on the topics that interest you and your family:

- Federal Citizen Information Center (www.pueblo .gsa.gov)
- FireSafety (www.firesafety.gov)
- Home Safety Council (www.homesafetycouncil.org)
- National Institutes of Health (www.nih.gov)
- The National Park Service (www.cr.nps.gov)
- WebMD (www.webmd.com)

Information changes daily and new resources become available all the time. Be sure to check your other favorite resources periodically for the latest and greatest materials available to you!

Chapter 17
Travel

*S*ummer vacations used to mean pinching pennies throughout the year. Not anymore, now that we take advantage of the insider tips and low rates on the Web.

—Alicia, *Utah*

You've scrimped, you've saved, and you've been crowned bargain queen of the year. What's next? Well, how about a vacation? Go on, take a trip, but don't let your shopping savvy fly out the window while you're preparing for your hiatus.

By following the information provided throughout this book, you will be able to prepare for your trip more cost-effectively. The savings won't stop there though; we've also included our collection of smart travel ideas to help. This chapter provides tips such as finding cheaper airfare and the best ways to eat out for less while on the road.

Destinations

Now that you've decided to take that well-deserved break, where will you decide to go? Whether you already have a destination in mind or need to scope out possibilities, there are a number of paths to get you there. Here are some hints for finding your perfect destination while enjoying the road along the way.

■ **Vacationing on a budget?** These sites offer tips and information about potential destinations:

- About Budget Travel (www.budgettravel .about.com)
- Backpack Europe on a Budget (www.back packeurope.com)
- Living a Better Life e-zine (www.betterbud geting.com/travel.htm)

■ **Looking for adventure?** Take a look around these websites for information on adventurous vacations:

- Planet Charters (www.planetcharters.com)
- Wide Open Spaces (www.wideopenspaces .co.uk)
- Adventure Women (www.adventurewomen .com)
- Adventure Travel (www.2adventure.com)

■ **Want a prime spot on the beach?** These websites will be of interest to you:

- Dr. Beach (www.drbeach.org)
- TBO.com Beaches (www.beaches.tbo.com)

- A World Tour of Beaches (www.allbeaches .net)
- SurfSun.com Beach Vacation Guide (www .surfsun.com)

■ **Do theme parks catch your interest?** A family vacation centered around a theme park attraction can provide a variety of fun for everyone. Visit these websites to gather information and tips for some popular destinations:

- Theme Park Insider (www.themeparkinsider .com)
- Ultimate Rollercoaster (www.ultimateroller coaster.com)
- Theme Parks Online (www.themeparkson line.org)
- Six Flags (www.sixflags.com)
- Disney Online (www.disney.com)
- Universal Studios (www.themeparks.universal studios.com)

Once you've settled on a particular destination, be sure to read Chapter 18 for ideas on finding free or low-cost activities in the area you've chosen.

Another important part of choosing a destination is finding the perfect place to stay. Unless you will be residing with friends or family, using the information available on the Internet will help you choose the best accommodations. There's a wealth of information on facilities and pricing available at the click of your mouse. Here are a few websites to get you started:

- Hotels.com (www.hotels.com)
- All-Hotels (www.all-hotels.com)
- Motels.com (www.motels.com)

- EscapeRental (www.escaperental.com)
- CondoRentals (www.condorentals.com)
- ResortFinder (www.resortfinder.com)
- Resorts and Lodges Travel Guide (www.resortsand lodges.com)

Keep in mind that if you are traveling by air, you may be able to receive a discount on your hotel and rental vehicles if you book all three services together. Determine where you'd like to stay and then check into your air and auto transportation options for available discounts prior to booking your accommodations.

Transportation

You've chosen the perfect spot, you've checked out the facilities; now it's time to find the best way to get from here to there. Let's explore the numerous methods of travel and how to save on each.

Plane

If you choose to travel by air, always shop around for the best prices. Use the following websites to begin gathering information, and perhaps later on, to book your trip:

- Travelocity (www.travelocity.com)
- Orbitz (www.orbitz.com)
- Expedia.com (www.expedia.com)
- Priceline.com (www.priceline.com)
- CheapTickets (www.cheaptickets.com)

It's also a good idea to visit the actual airline websites such as Delta Airlines (www.delta.com) to see what discount airfare options they may have available. Sometimes you will find a better price purchasing directly from the airline than you will on a discount website. Also, check for military, student, group, or senior discounts if applicable, as some airlines may offer these.

Don't forget to use any frequent flier miles you may have accumulated through a special promotion or credit card offer. Some credit cards may also have special discount offers with certain airlines, so be sure to find out about all of your options before purchasing your tickets.

Train

Traveling to your destination by train may be a cheaper alternative and a fun experience for your family. Viewing the countryside from the comfort of a train has its appeal. Here are some websites to get you started in your quest to find available train routes:

- Amtrak (www.amtrak.com)
- TrainWeb (www.trainweb.com)
- TheTrainLine (www.thetrainline.com)
- USA by Rail (www.usa-by-rail.com)
- European Rail Guide (www.europeanrailguide.com)

Bus

Whether you are going short or long distances, there may be a bus tour or route available to get you there. Check out this convenient form of travel at the following websites:

- Greyhound (www.greyhound.com)
- Tour Vacations To Go (www.tourvactationstogo.com)
- Gray Line (www.grayline.com)
- Affordable Tours (www.affordabletours.com)

Automobile

If you aren't traveling by road to begin with, you may need a rental vehicle when you arrive at your destination. Here are a few websites that may help you along your way:

- Auto Europe (www.autoeurope.com)
- CarRental.net (www.carrental.net)
- CarRental.com (www.carrental.com)
- EV Rental Cars (www.evrental.com)
- Recreation Vehicle Rental Association (www.rvra .org)

Consider renting a smaller vehicle to save some cash. Remember, you are only using this vehicle on your vacation, so if your family is small, you can save money by renting a compact rather than an SUV.

Remember, if you are flying or booking a hotel reservation, you may find a related discount offered on your rental vehicle. Be sure to wait until you have all your plans solidified before booking your rental, as you'll want to take advantage of the best offers available.

Ship

Are you beckoned by the call of the sea? Your perfect dream vacation may be on the water. Investigate your options beginning with the following websites:

- SmartCruiser (www.smartcruiser.com)
- Cruise.com (www.cruise.com)
- Cruise Lines International Association (www.cruising .org)
- The Ferry Traveller (www.ferrytravel.com)
- Ferry Companies of the Web (www.ferrytravel.de)

Dining and Entertainment

Arranging for your destination accommodations and transportation is half the battle. Once you arrive at your vacation spot, you'll have dining, entertainment, souvenir, and other expenses to consider as well. No worries though—you are an expert who's already equipped with the tools to save, even while on vacation. We've listed some additional ideas here to help you stretch your vacation dollars enough to stay an extra day or two!

Pick a Souvenir

Every vacation spot vendor knows souvenirs are a huge cash pot. Before you spend your dollars on trinkets and T-shirts, consider whether you'll really use them when the vacation is over. One thrifty and fun idea is to pick one particular type of item and build a collection over time. For example, if you are a coffee lover, collect coffee cups from your vacation spots. Make it your mission to find unique or handcrafted mugs on each trip. In the end, you'll have a useful collection of memories and money in your pocket.

Have you decided to take the kids to a licensed theme park like Disney? While everyone loves choosing their own souvenirs, those licensed goodies can cost a fortune. Consider picking up some small items, such as magnets and pens, locally before your trip. Pack them in your luggage when your children are not around. Then each day, you can leave one souvenir on their pillow, making the most of their vacation, while saving yourself a bundle.

Dine with Discounts

Even if you've never been to the area before, you can still dine for less. Call the hotel you will be staying at or ask friends who live in the area, including your online forum friends, what restaurants you should try. Also, search for local web pages on your particular vacation spot to find restaurant information. Two websites to try are Dine.com (www.dine.com) and the United States Restaurant Guide (www.usrg.com).

After you've identified the places you'd like to try, run a search on the restaurants to see whether their websites offer special promotions or coupons. There are also more general websites that offer discount options to eateries in a variety of locales. Here are a few you may want to try:

- Restaurant.com (www.restaurant.com)
- DinnerBroker (www.dinnerbroker.com)
- CoolSavings (www.coolsavings.com)
- Valpak.com (www.valpak.com)

You may also want to pick up a local newspaper when you arrive at your destination; it may contain discount coupons for popular restaurants and services. Want the paper ahead of time? Run a search on newspapers for the area you'll be visiting, such as "Orlando FL newspaper," and see how much it costs to have a copy of the most recent edition sent to your home in advance.

A Few More Quick Tips for Travel

Here's some more "insider" information that we just have to pass on.

■ **Find out what your memberships have to offer.** Organizations like the America Automobile Association (AAA) may offer discount vacation packages for members. Your employer or credit union may have similar programs. Take a look at your memberships and find out what they have to offer in the vacation arena; you may be pleasantly surprised to find a great deal on the trip of your dreams.

- **Leave the credit cards at home.** Obviously you will want to have one with you in case of an emergency, but don't bring a wallet full of credit cards. Instead, consider bringing a limited amount of traveler's checks, an ATM card, or a pre-paid bank card (such as a Visa check card). Impulse spending is what vacations are all about. Set a budget and stick to it. It's okay to splurge a little, but you don't want to go overboard.

- **Ask around.** See what your Internet pals, friends, and family know about your destination. They may know about sites and attractions that are off the beaten path. Perhaps there is a small museum or historical library you wouldn't want to miss. Maybe there is a small town right outside of the city you are visiting that's worth a side trip. You can add some wonderful memories to your vacation when you tap into insider information.

- **Packing tips.** Packing can be a traveler's biggest headache. Make a list of the things you will need, and check them off as they go into your suitcases. This will help curb avoidable expenses, such as a new toothbrush, once you have reached your destination.

- **Consider an off-season vacation.** Traveling during the off-season has it advantages. Often the weather and other pluses of the location are just as nice, and sometimes even better than traveling during peak times. Hotels and other attractions may offer discounted rates during the off-season to draw more tourists, so it's worth considering.

Chapter 18

Entertainment

L iving in a rural location used to limit our access to other gamers who share similar passions. Now they are only a click away.

—DAWN, *Idaho*

Keeping the family entertained on a budget is not as hard as you might think. You have already learned so much throughout this book that we are confident you can apply those skills to every aspect of your life, including entertainment at and away from home.

Use the information in this chapter as a quick guide to help you save your money and your sanity while keeping your loved ones content throughout the year.

Books

Watching television night after night can get old quick. Stimulate your family members' minds and imaginations with the wonderful world of books instead. Whether it's an e-book, a paperback, or a hardcover, the wonders of the literary world are yours to explore at the turn of a page. Check these websites for reviews, contests, and other goodies sure to keep your family happy and entertained on those rainy, nothing-to-do sort of days:

- Barb Webb (www.barbwebb.com)
- Free-eBooks (www.free-ebooks.net)
- The eBook Directory (www.ebookdirectory.com)
- The New York Times Book Reviews (www.nytimes.com/pages/books)
- Barnes and Noble (www.barnesandnoble.com)
- BookSpot (www.bookspot.com)

Looking to save money on your favorite titles? Try these tips to maximize your savings while searching for the perfect read.

■ **Compare.** Check out your favorite price comparison websites before purchasing any reading material to ensure that you get the best possible price.

■ **Trade.** Did you just finish a really good read? Let your online buds know. Ask them what they are reading and if they are willing to trade books with you. Consider using the U.S. Postal Service if your items fall within the USPS guidelines. Use media mail when shipping to maximize your savings. Just don't trade your copy of this book; you wouldn't want to get caught without it.

■ **Discount book stores.** Check with sites like Amazon (www.amazon.com) and Half.com (www.half.com) for used copies of the books you are interested in reading. You never know what you may find.

When you read an exceptional book, be sure to take a few minutes and review it on your favorite websites. Reviews are invaluable to those considering a purchase, and your review could tip the scales one way or the other for many potential readers.

■ **Get a library card.** There is always plenty to read at the library—and best of all, it's free. The only requirements are a library card and a promise to return the book in a timely fashion.

■ **Consider e-book alternatives.** E-book websites are rising in popularity due to the shorter length of stories, variety of subject matter, and low purchase prices. Look around for websites that match your reading interests and you may find some entertaining alternatives.

Movies

Get the popcorn; we're going to watch a movie. This section will help you save money when watching movies at home or in the theater.

Here are a few sites that offer reviews on new and older movies so you can evaluate them before bringing them home.

- ScreenIt.com (www.screenit.com)
- Kids-in-Mind (www.kids-in-mind.com)
- FamilyStyle Film Guide (www.familystyle.com)
- RogerEbert.com (www.rogerebert.suntimes.com)

■ **DVD/VHS clubs.** If your family watches a lot of movies, DVD/VHS clubs may be just right for you. You get to choose several movies at minimal cost with the promise of making a set amount of purchases within a predetermined amount of time. Be sure to read the terms and conditions thoroughly before committing to any programs. Also check out Columbia House (www.columbiahouse.com) for both music and movie clubs, as well as Disney Movie Club (www.disney .videos.go.com).

■ **Trade**. Trade DVDs within your online communities to help expand your entertainment possibilities. You can trade short term or permanently—it's up to you.

■ **Rental clubs**. You may want to consider joining a DVD rental club, where you select movies from a list and then receive and return your selections via postal mail. Again, carefully read the terms and conditions before joining these clubs. If you only watch two movies per month, a rental club may not be economically sound for you. Check out Netflix (www.netflix.com), Blockbuster Online (www.blockbuster.com), and Greencine (www.greencine.com) for more information about their rental programs.

■ **Download**. A new trend in home entertainment is the ability to download movies onto your computer. It's a reasonably priced alternative. Movies can be viewed on your computer, laptop, or television. For more information, check out websites like Movielink (www.movielink.com) or Ultimate Movie Download (www.ultimatemoviedownload.com).

■ **Library**. Libraries are not just about books; they also carry a nice selection of videos for your family's enjoyment. Check it out.

Going out to the movies? Look up your movie theater information online. Also, be sure to check with your local cinemas for promotions or coupons on tickets or concessions. Here are a few theater-related websites to get you started:

- Yahoo! Movies (www.movies.yahoo.com)
- Moviefone (www.movies.channel.aol.com)
- Regal Entertainment Group (www.regalcinemas.com)
- Landmark Theatres (www.landmarktheatres.com)
- AMC Theatres (www.amctheatres.com)
- Cinemark (www.cinemark.com)
- Loews Cineplex (www.enjoytheshow.com)
- Sony IMAX (www.imax.com)

Games and Sports

Games are a wonderful form of entertainment. Whether you choose to play an online game or a family board game, it is a surefire way to have some fun.

Online gaming has become a huge part of the Internet experience. There are multiple- and single-player games, role playing, strategy, card, and just plain silly games—all out there waiting for you to find. Don't know how to play chess? Go to chess.about.com to learn. Are you a Scrabble nut? Take on your friends and family in an online tournament using the Internet Scrabble Club (www.isc.ro). Do you prefer to play alone? Try games like Word Whomp or Bookworm. To find these games and others, visit Shockwave.com (www.shockwave.com), or type "free Internet games" into your favorite search engine. You won't be disappointed by these single player freebies.

Warning: The following websites are highly addictive, so have fun at your own risk:

- MSN Games (www.zone.com)
- Yahoo! Games (www.games.yahoo.com)
- Pogo (www.pogo.com)
- Game Rival (www.gamerival.com)

Some of these gaming sites have pay options as well. Purchasing a membership will allow you access to more features and levels than the free memberships provide. Weigh your options, and decide whether a paid membership is something you could benefit from.

Remember, your PC has built-in games too. Solitaire is just a click away whether you are using Microsoft Windows or one of the other latest and greatest operating systems. Check with your software manufacturer for details. You may also find additional games available for free download on the manufacturer's website.

Video games are not just for consoles and TVs anymore. You can play on one of the many state-of-the-art systems or on your PC. Just be sure to read the system requirements and check for compatibility before spending your cash to sign up.

Check out these sites for reviews and deals on PC software and video games:

- GameSpot (www.gamespot.com)
- Yahoo! Games Domain (www.gamesdomain.yahoo .com)
- Freeware Home (www.freewarehome.com)

Some additional hints for increasing the fun factor in your gaming experience:

■ **Watch for sales.** Sites like Amazon.com often have buy-one-get-one-free sales on board games and low prices on video games or PC software. Check these sites often to see what they offer, and you will be sure to find a bargain. You will usually find last year's hot games deeply discounted as new games are released on the market.

■ **Check your online communities.** Maybe a member of your community is looking to unload the software titles her children no longer use. You may be able to arrange a trade or sale and add to your entertainment selections in the same way as you sell or trade books, movies, or clothes.

■ **Watch your newsletters.** Newsletters often contain discounts off future purchases, making your new software purchases that much sweeter. You could save 20 percent or $15 off your next purchase, so don't let those savings slip away.

■ **Check your auction sites.** You may find just what you are looking for at a price that's difficult to resist.

■ **Join online gaming communities.** You may meet new friends who have similar interests or find great bargains on used games. Some popular websites are:

- Boardgame Players Association (www.board gamers.org)
- Million Minute Family Challenge (www .millionminute.com)
- GameNight (www.gamenight.com)
- Games Talks (www.gamestalks.com)

You'll find plenty of information to satisfy all your gaming needs for a very long time.

Want to play outside? No problem. Use your savvy shopping skills to find gear at rock-bottom prices. Whether it's a new helmet for your dirt bike racing enthusiast or a lure for your fisherman, the family outdoorsman will never suffer by having you in the house.

Check out these sites for some great information and deals for all your outside activities:

- The Sportsman's Guide (www.sportsmansguide.com)
- Bargain Outfitters (www.bargainoutfitters.com)
- Sierra Trading Post (www.sierratradingpost.com)
- HuntingNet (www.hunting.net)
- Cabela's (www.cabelas.com)
- Motoworld Racing (www.motoworldracing.com)

Local Activities

Most communities offer a ton of fun things for residents to enjoy. Check with your state's website to see what they offer for local entertainment. They may raffle or give away tickets or offer discounts to local businesses and restaurants. Here are a few other ways to find out what's going on.

- **Listen to your local radio programs.** They often give away tickets to concerts, sporting events, and shows. Call in or participate in their online contests. You may be a lucky winner.

■ **Visit your city online.** Find your city or chamber of commerce website by typing your city and state into your favorite search engine. You're bound to pull up a wealth of information about the area and links to attractions, parks, and other interesting activities.

■ **Check your online communities.** People who live in the same area as you may have tickets to see a children's show or passes to a movie they are unable to attend. You could potentially pick up these tickets for a song or may even get them for free.

■ **Take advantage of free or low-fee government- or state-sponsored facilities.** You may have national park facilities near you with hiking trails, picnic spots, lakes, beaches, and a whole lot more. Visit the National Park Service website (www.nps.gov) or US-Parks (www.us-parks.com) to find out what you might have in your backyard.

■ **Check on access to local museums, zoos, or cultural centers.** Many of these facilities offer free admission or periodic reduced admissions to local residents. For more information, check out the following websites:

- The American Zoo and Aquarium Association (www.aza.org)
- ZooWeb (www.zooweb.com)
- The International Council of Museums (www.icom.museum)
- Free-Attractions (www.free-attractions.com)

Miscellaneous Fun

No matter what avenue you choose to explore, there's a ton of fun to be had on the Internet. Check out these websites for some wacky entertainment. We would like to warn you up front that some of these websites may contain material that is unsuitable for children, so use caution when exploring them for the first time.

- Fark.com (www.fark.com)
- JoeCartoon (www.joecartoon.atomfilms.com)
- JibJab (www.jibjab.com)
- LaughNet (www.laughnet.net)
- Snopes (www.snopes.com)
- Humorsource.com (www.humorsource.com)
- Pet Humor (www.pethumor.com)

Afterword

Congratulations! You are now ready to take the cyberworld by storm. Regardless of your Internet knowledge and skill level when you picked up this book for the first time, you now have all of the information necessary to surf the Net like a pro. Anything is possible if you just put your mind to it, and with a little bit of time and effort, the sky is the limit.

You may have noticed that we, the authors, live in different states. Interestingly enough, through this entire experience from idea to print, we've never met even once face-to-face. So how was it possible for us to create such a fun and informative book with a distance of eight-hundred-plus miles between us?

The dream became reality thanks to a strong friendship built and nurtured online, along with the endless possibilities presented by the Internet. We "met" by posting on our favorite online freebies board—the Fugee Forums (www.fugeeforums .com)—and became fast friends.

Not only did we share similar interests, including a love of freebies and some serious bargain hunting skills, but we found out we were both writers. After exchanging e-mails and critiquing each other's material, we found our work was complementary and decided to engage in a venture together as a team.

We've put a lot of hard work and effort into the pages of this book in the hopes that many other women across the country will reap the same benefits on the Internet that we have. No matter how much you earn or save using the Web as your tool, the friendships you nurture will be absolutely priceless, ones you will cherish for years to come. We wish everyone the same blessings our friendship has brought us.

We've done our best to prepare and encourage you, and you may be asking, "What now?" Simple, take the knowledge presented in this book, and use it to wow your friends and family with your shopping savvy and moneymaking skills. You now have all the necessary tools required to earn money on the Web, as well as the ability to obtain all the creature comforts desired by your family without straying outside the confines of your budget. It's up to you to put them to good use.

Whether you decide to participate in surveys, mystery shop, use your bargain hunting skills, or become an online entrepreneur, you can be successful when you follow the guidelines presented in this book. We strongly believe no matter what path you choose to pursue online, the Internet will present a fun and rewarding experience that can only be enhanced by what you have learned within the pages of this guide.

Be sure to visit momdotcom.net often for more tips and tricks to keep you up-to-date on the latest Internet trends. You will find additional resources, lots of printables, and other information pertinent to your Internet experience. We'd love to have you sign our guestbook and share your success stories with us! We look forward to hearing from you.

Happy surfing!

Glossary

Browser A software program that provides the main porthole through which you gain entry to the Internet. Used to view web pages and computer files.

Chat Room An Internet relay chat (IRC) that allows real-time interactive online discussions between Internet users and groups. Users typically use text messaging to carry on a conversation. Everyone in the chat room has the capability to read the text and respond. Some chat room technology also allows for voice conferencing.

Cookie A packet of information sent by a website to your browser. The browser saves information such as your log-in, user preferences, and other identification to the cookie. Each time you access the website, the cookie is read. This allows companies to use the information stored in the cookie to custom tailor content to your tastes, keep a log of your activity, or grant you quicker access to the website.

Cyberspace Generally used as an alternate term for the Internet. Also used to describe the travel route of information over the Internet.

Domain Name A name designated to an Internet website, such as momdotcom.net or momdotcom.info.

Download   The transfer of files or data from one computer to another.

E-mail   Short for electronic mail; electronic messages sent from one computer user to another or to multiple users, typically transferred using the Internet.

Forum   An Internet website established for the purpose of sharing information with other Internet users. Information is posted (saved) to the website so that other users may read/view it and respond.

HTML   Acronym for hypertext markup language, the coding language of the Web. It allows for a common standard of text coding to let browsers properly read and view web pages.

Internet   A worldwide connection of telecommunications and computer networks that allows users to share information and converse with other Internet users. Originally established to create fast access to information for research purposes, the Internet is now used for any number of practical purposes, including research, communication, and commerce.

ISP   The acronym for Internet service provider, a business that provides an access route to the Internet, usually for a fee.

Link   An interactive point on a web page that allows you to access another area of the website or a different website altogether.

Net   Slang for the Internet.

Netiquette   Slang for etiquette used on the Internet.

Search Engine   A web-based database system used for finding information on the Internet.

Spam   Commonly referred to as "electronic junk mail." Spam is considered to be any unsolicited e-mail sent without the consent or permission of the recipient.

URL   Acronym for uniform resource locator, the electronic address identifying a particular website or web page (for example, www.momdotcom.net).

Web   Short for World Wide Web.

Web page   A document designed for the purpose of being read by a browser. A website is typically made of one or more web pages.

Website   A compilation of information (such as text, images, and sound) contained on electronic documents commonly referred to as web pages.

WWW   Acronym for the World Wide Web, a collection of websites designed to be viewed through a standard browser. The WWW is not the entire Internet, but a portion of it.

Additional Resources

Though numerous resources are mentioned throughout this guide, the following is a list of additional mom-friendly organizations and sites that may be helpful to you.

Administration for Children & Families
370 L'Enfant Promenade, S.W.
Washington, DC 20201
www.headstartinfo.org

Better Business Bureau
www.bbb.org

Family and Home Network
www.familyandhome.org

Family Life
www.familylife.com

Federal Trade Commission
600 Pennsylvania Ave., N.W.
Washington, DC 20580
www.ftc.gov

Hearts at Home
900 West College
Normal, IL 61761
www.hearts-at-home.org

International Moms Club
25371 Rye Canyon
Valencia, CA 91355
www.momsclub.org

Modern Mom, LLC
10940 Wilshire Blvd., Ste. 1600
Los Angeles, CA 90024
(310) 443-4232
www.modernmom.com

Mothers & More
P.O. Box 31
Elmhurst, IL 60126
www.mothersandmore.org

Mothers of Preschoolers (MOPS)
2370 S. Trenton Way
Denver, CO 80231
www.gospelcom.net/mops

National Do Not Call Registry
www.donotcall.gov

National Institutes of Health
9000 Rockville Pike
Bethesda, MD 20892
www.nih.gov

Parents Helping Parents
www.php.com

The Partnership for Reading
c/o National Institute for Literacy
1775 I St. N.W., Suite 730
Washington, DC 20006
www.nifl.gov/partnershipforreading

United States Department of Health and Human Services
200 Independence Ave., S.W.
Washington, DC 20201
www.surgeongeneral.gov

Urban Legends Reference Pages
www.snopes.com

USDA Food, Nutrition, and Consumer Services
U.S. Department of Agriculture
1400 Independence Ave., S.W.
Washington, DC 20250
www.fns.usda.gov

Working Moms Refuge
www.momsrefuge.com

Index

About the Authors

With a background in computer technology, education, marketing, and promotional communications, **Barb Webb** has written over two hundred curriculum manuals for the corporate sector and has published numerous short stories, poems, and articles. In addition, Webb is an editor for Chippewa Publishing Ltd., the founder and owner of MOMdotCOM.net, and a regular columnist for *Suite* magazine. In recognition of her writing and work with the community, Webb received the 1999 Professional Association of Computer Training (PACT) First Place Award of Excellence and the 1999 Minnesota Children and Family Services Volunteer of the Year Award.

Maureen Heck is content editor for www.fugeeforums.com, an online community for moms to exchange information and ideas. She also actively participates in parenting and general debate boards and has over eight years Internet experience. Her thirteen years in the grocery industry gave her thorough knowledge of retail, which helps in her endeavors with MOMdot COM.net. Choosing to leave the manager mentoring program at her job to raise her daughter and pursue her writing, Heck is currently a stay at home mom, residing in New Jersey with her daughter, husband, and black Lab. While this is her first publication, Heck is pursuing a career in fiction writing.